Speaking From The Heart

Speaking From The Heart

Essays on being the Church of Scotland

Marjory A MacLean

Shoving Leopard

First published in 2010 by

Shoving Leopard
Flat 2F3, 8 Edina Street
Edinburgh
EH7 5PN
United Kingdom
http://www.shovingleopard.com/

ISBN 978 1 905565 16 0

A catalogue record for this book is available from the British Library.

Foreword

These neatly observed portraits and insightfully crafted essays come from the pen of one who is extremely well placed to comment on the people and politics which make up the Church of Scotland at the end of the first decade of the twenty-first century.

A native of Forfar, Marjory MacLean studied Law at Edinburgh University, qualifying as a solicitor and practising in Kirkwall. After sensing a call to ministry she returned to Edinburgh, gaining a first class honours degree in divinity. This was followed by probationary training at Fairmilehead Parish Church, during which time she was appointed to the Unity. Faith and Order Commission of the newly created Action of Churches Together in Scotland (ACTS). In 1992 she returned to Orkney as parish minister in Stromness where she served until 1998. In 1996 she was appointed Depute Clerk of the General Assembly, initially combining what was then a part time role with her parish ministry. From 1998 until 2010 she has served as full time Depute Clerk and acted as Principal Clerk of the General Assemblies of 2002, 2003 and 2009. In 2009 she was Minutes Clerk to the Assembly of the Conference of European Churches meeting at Lyons in France She has clerked and been a consistent supporter of the Church of Scotland Youth Assembly encouraging its evolution over recent years. She has taught church law, practice and procedure to candidates for the ministry and has assisted the Ecumenical Relations Committee in the intricacies of legal issues relating to local ecumenical partnerships. She has been a valued member of the Joint Commission on Doctrine of the Church of Scotland and the Roman Catholic Church.

In 2004 she was awarded a PhD from Edinburgh University for a thesis entitled *The Crown Rights of the Redeemer: A Reformed Approach to Sovereignty for the National Church in the 21st Century*, and built on this research in her widely acclaimed Chalmers Lectures of 2007-08. These were published in expanded form in 2009 as *The Crown Rights of the Redeemer: The Spiritual Freedom of the Church of Scotland,* and offer a contemporary assessment of the Church's constitutional arrangements in relation to wider society. Also in 2009 she edited a collection of essays published by Dundee University Press under the title *The Legal Systems of Scottish Churches* and this is proving a most useful resource for lawyers appearing before church courts.

Since 2004 she has been a Royal Naval Reserve Chaplain attached to HMS SCOTIA at Rosyth and from mid 2010 she will be operationally deployed as a full time Naval Chaplain during a period of mobilisation.

In this slim volume Dr MacLean draws on the considerable experience represented by all of these strands and the reader will find much on which to reflect. In these pages lies material which will challenge and inform, observations which will amuse and perhaps even irritate. And those with the gift to see themselves as other see them may recognise themselves and discern something of their journeys towards ministry, the workings of their kirk sessions or presbyteries, their handling of pastoral situations, the manner and effectiveness of their Christian witness.

One of the many joys of my tenure of the office of Principal Clerk has been the opportunity to work closely with such an immensely able colleague. I am grateful for that and warmly commend this volume to the Church and all who care about it.

Finlay Macdonald
May, 2010

Contents

Introduction

Writing a reference for a friend is a delicate task. She has asked you to do it because she supposes you may be warmly disposed to her and keen to help her secure the position she wants. She is expecting you to be positive, and to recommend her for the post. Meanwhile by agreeing to do it you have cast yourself into a position of responsibility to the employer, to whom you have a moral duty to be honest and let them know of concerns they ought to investigate or hesitations they ought to consider. Some referees resolve this dilemma of conscience by persuading themselves that a painfully honest reference is in fact a kindness to its subject, since it will presumably help to avoid her ending up in a job where she would be useless and miserable – it is a form of the 'be cruel to be kind' argument. Other referees, especially if they are worried that the reference will be seen by the applicant and the friendship damaged as a result, will make a pointed offer in the text to discuss by telephone any other questions the employer may have, hoping the reader can take the hint, make the call and discover the awful truth.

The pieces that make up this small collection might be likened to a reference for the Church of Scotland considered as a social institution. They are written by a minister who could not be fonder of the Church, and I did hesitate once or twice before setting down some of my more blunt and critical comments. However, there is no realistic opportunity for every reader to make that discreet telephone call to acquire the killer information afterwards; so into the text it has all had to go. Just a word to disappoint the reader: except where someone is actually named, there are no descriptions of single individuals anywhere in the texts. I have, in other words, concentrated on recurring irritations, and those generate composite pictures.

These essays have all been written during Lent 2010, just after my departure from the post of Depute Clerk to the Church's General Assembly. For the latter eleven years of that appointment I was based in the Principal Clerk's Department in the Church Offices, and by far the biggest element of my work was responding to phone calls and e-mails asking for procedural advice, information about church law, or suggestions for dealing with disputes or complaints that had gone beyond the possibility of informal resolution. A smaller element of the job, but among the most delightful, was teaching our Church Law course to probationer ministers and others in training.

The material in this little book, where it seems to offer advice, is largely a distilling of the suggestions I most often made in those two capacities of consultant and teacher. Not so much the Frequently Asked Questions as the Frequently Given Answers.

I have chosen to write the major items in this volume as essays. It seems to be a form of writing that has faded in our generation, surviving mainly in the form of opinion pieces in broadsheet newspapers or brief blog-posts on the internet. It has been interesting for me, and I hope stimulating for the reader, to reflect at some leisure on a series of connected themes. Each essay will be read in no more than twice the time it takes to hear a sermon; and I rather hope that will reassure the sort of readership I suspect they might have.

Virginia Woolf, writing essays about essay-writing, expressed strong and particular opinions about the art. She believed that the essay is 'primarily an expression of personal opinion' and that almost all essays begin with a capital 'I'.[1] The essays in this book fulfil the first part of that characterisation, with no apology on my part. However, Woolf also believed that the essay should be designed for a single, simple purpose:[2]

'The principle that controls it is simply that it should give pleasure; the desire which impels us when we take it from the shelf is simply to receive pleasure. Everything in an essay must be subdued to that end.'

Here I confess to a less singular motivation. There are essays in the following pages that are written in a reflective style, designed to provide pleasure but also provocation, and to inspire conversation and discussion around the Church: for example 'Organised Religion'. Were they to give unalloyed pleasure I would suspect they were not as useful as I had hoped. There are other essays here that by no stretch of a generous imagination could be mistaken for works of literature; they were written only to inform and assist, and they use the casual style that seemed to work when I was teaching groups within the Church: 'The First-Time Commissioner' is an obvious example.

[1] The Decay of Essay-Writing, in *Selected Essays,* Oxford: Oxford University Press 2008 p. 4
[2] The Modern Essay, ibid. p.13

There are some individuals, though, who I hope will simply take pleasure in this book, and these I will gladly name.

The Principal Clerk's Department – soon to become the Department of the General Assembly – is probably one of the best vantage-points from which to observe how the Church of Scotland works. From the top floor of 121 George Street one can see the best and worst of the Church; the figurative view is as extensive as the panorama from the window. This volume tries to describe a few aspects of that institutional landscape in terms that will be perfectly familiar to any Church insider; but like a painting it offers an interpretation its readers will need to think about, and which they will like or dislike according to taste and experience. The book comes with love to Linda, Alison and Pauline up there on the fourth floor, who will be providing continuity in this year of changes; and it comes with my very best wishes to John and Pauline as they join the team and plan its new directions.

I have not included any essays about the central administration of the Church, and that will come as a disappointment to some readers who would be curious about such things, and a relief to many who know they have better things to do with their time than peer into that piece of machinery. There is one thing, though, that must be recorded.

Finlay Macdonald retires in June 2010 after fourteen years as Principal Clerk to the General Assembly and, very significantly, as Secretary to the various manifestations of the Council of Assembly that have come and gone in that time. The central administration of the Church has been transformed, always with his guidance and advice, from the largely uncoordinated and expensive collection of agencies suitable for the Church of a previous generation, into an increasingly lean, coordinated and highly accountable executive function. As a young man, Finlay was attracted to several different professions, including lawyer, minister, politician and diplomat. As he retires, he can be content that he has been the best of each of those in bringing such extensive and necessary reform to the institution he cares about so deeply.

Selfishly I will always be most grateful for the opportunities, support and companionship he has given me in during that strange slice of my career now ended. So with love to him and Elma, I dedicate this book to Finlay.

Marjory A MacLean
Easter 2010

Pen portrait

He cannot take his eyes off her, and it gives him quite a knot in his stomach to watch her because it has put a life-changing thought into his mind.

No, no, nothing like that.

Back home with his parents it was clear enough how he went to church. It was part of the pattern of the week and it changed as little as the landscape around the village. The minister had been there as long as he could remember, and was a nice guy in his 60s who knew nothing about the telly you watched or the web-sites you surfed or the games you played – but that didn't matter. A nice guy who wasn't embarrassed by a teenager crying when Gran died; a nice guy who kind of made Bible stories sound as if they were talking about stuff you still worried about; a nice guy who really went out of his way to save the village nursery when it was threatened with closure. And then the Youth Group had been part of the ordinary week for the last four years. You went along, you fitted in, you didn't stand out, you did the Bible studies or you went to the barbeques or you signed up for the weekend trips; and it was all stuff arranged for you. Church just happened, really.

And you'd think that coming to this Church round the corner from the Halls of Residence would be sort of re-assuring, something a bit like home now that home is suddenly rather far away. There might be a group to join, something for new students, something that would carry on arranging church stuff for you to do. He had hoped before he came that there might be a minister like his own one, somebody he could feel able to speak to if things went a bit pear-shaped during the term. It would be good just to carry on with what he knew, you know?

But there she is, just five years old than himself, and they call her the attached student. She is actually training to be a minister, at her age, looking like that, dressing like that. She knows about music and telly and films. She has the guts to get up and do the prayers sometimes, and next week she'll be doing the sermon at the evening service. She is way too much like him and his friends; and he can't keep his astonished eyes off her. Church is suddenly a whole different kettle of fish, and that is an uncomfortable thought.

And the life-changing thought... Maybe there is an answer to that puzzle of what you do with a degree in English and History.

Maybe the people at home who keep telling him how good he is with other people, what a deep thinker he is about serious issues, maybe they are getting at something. Maybe he needs to ask her if she has time for a coffee some time, to tell him how she's ended up doing this, here, now. What does it take? Would they laugh too much at home? Does he care?

Power in the congregation

If ever there existed a social organism that would repay psychological or systems-theory scrutiny, it would be a good-sized Church of Scotland congregation. For a body called to be a single spiritual entity and designed to achieve laudable tasks, a congregation often seems rather to be a fascinating web of relationships and dynamics, and some of them can seem competitive and stressful.

The human yearning for control

Human insecurity is one of the fundamental problems we spend our lives trying to overcome. It seems to be part of our original condition, as if part of the punishment for that distant ancestral horror that Christians tell and re-tell because it comforts us as we try to make sense of the ultimate inadequacy of even the best of us. The sinister suspicion we each have that we live dangerously close to a loss of control over our circumstances – at any moment accident, bereavement, someone else's terrible mistake or our own overwhelming temptation could drag us into a most terrifying new existence – makes us maximise the comfort and confidence we have in our present surroundings, because then we feel less vulnerable.

Any human institution provides a finite environment which provides the same anxieties and needs, and in which we play out the strategies of coping with uncertainty and weakness. An organisation has a membership, a structure, a way of operating, a way of regulating the routine and non-routine events in its corporate life. An organisation has roles for people, things for them to achieve; it has, in other words, ways for a person to be someone, something. Each human institution, to some varying extent, provides a setting for human beings to enact those relationships of power and control which meet such a visceral need in each poor one of us.

The Church paints that environment, those opportunities, its structures and activities, in very bright colours indeed. The Church offers to engage with people deep below most of their outer layers of confidence, cheerfulness and coping, and reaches in to the places where we keep our fears tucked away. The Church announces challenges to people that question those very parts of them, difficult challenges in the areas of principle, conduct, relationships, morality, spirituality. The Church appears to promise that the most fragile and unattractive characters of our human community will have an equal place and dignity amongst us. The Church, obeying its very purpose and mandate, sets itself up as the place above all others where the dynamics of personal power will be virtually uncontainable.

Church and the need for control

When a new minister arrives in a congregation, makes promises at his induction service and wakes up the next morning in his unfamiliar new manse, he is aware that he faces the now-famous quartet: known knowns, unknown knowns, known unknowns and unknown unknowns. The known knowns include the information he has been given, the research on the area he has been able to do, and the standard challenges and needs of every parish that will come as no surprise therefore in this one. The unknown knowns include his own ministerial formation and education, the mental and spiritual equipment that will sustain him without his always realising it, and the people he has not met but whose fears and griefs he already understands. The unknown unknowns await him behind closed doors in the parish, in the unexpected requests that will make him laugh or make him quake, in the achievements he will one day be proud of (but better to be in ignorance of them meantime).

The dynamics of power and fear, mixed up in so many of the people who are welcoming him to their congregation, provide one of the principal 'known unknowns' to the minister. He could see the people sitting in the pews at the induction service, but he has scarcely begun to figure out the wiring that really connects them. Some of it will be easy to uncover: who is related to whom by blood, marriage, friendship or intimacy. Some of it will be explicit: who engage with each other in recognised congregational groups, who share tasks. And the most important parts of it can only be discovered over a longer time spent there: where is trust, where is mistrust, who hogs tasks and who covets them, who has influence, who is marked for life by disappointment, what never works smoothly because the wrong combination of people collide every time. The wise minister knows all of these are there to be found, while the foolish one treats the congregation as if no-one is so human.

Task, status and ownership

If this network of connections and collisions of people is a kind of economy, then its currencies are task and status. This fallen human feels that this week she has a contribution to make because the flowers in the vestibule this Sunday will be ones she has put there and arranged. That fallen human has sat in the tenor section of the choir for forty years now, and is rightly conscious of the wonderful difference his voice has made to the praise of God in that place, and it is a natural part of how he thinks of himself and his worth. And this other fallen human looks at the pointing round the vestry window, and properly takes quiet satisfaction from her convenership of the property task group that decided to have that work done. And that fallen human over there is the auxiliary minister, and probably could not cope very well if she were not.

Sometimes, though, the task or the status becomes the kind of currency that people covet too much, and there develops a possessiveness, a territorial defensiveness, that spoils how people manage with each other. The property convener stops consulting the task group, and regards them as thoroughly ungrateful when they challenge the actions she has taken without their authority. The Session Clerk adjusts the minutes of the meeting to reflect what really should have been expressed there. The soprano whose voice has long since failed sits relentlessly in the front row of the choir and wordlessly defies the choirmaster to rescue the quality of the music by removing her. The minister changes the familiar practice of long years so fast that gentle souls are frightened to the core and lose any sense of religious security they ever knew. Each one of them, probably, is acting out of their own fears and inadequacies.

The organist, and others

The relationship of minister and organist is sometimes used to illustrate the problems. Each of them has their area of training and speciality, but each of them has been around the Church long enough to know quite a bit about the other's role and task. The organist often has a strong personal faith, and therefore has opinions about the whole service and not just its music; while the minister may happen to be musical enough to be able to think critically about the musical life of the worshipping community. They are regularly engaged together in a task with overlapping elements, trying to integrate what each can bring into a flowing sequence that will affect and effect the worship of others. They are constantly required to walk onto each other's territory, exchange the currency of their responsibilities, meet – and more than meet – each other and survive the meeting. Their relationship requires a level of trust and mutual respect that exists far more often than it is absent; and where it exists perhaps a small miracle must have happened every time.

An example as easy to understand as that one tells us that we must be capable of understanding how all sorts of people, encountering each other in the work of congregational life, may have the same difficulty. So it is not that organists are peculiarly unreasonable people, nor that ministers expect the worst from them and by expecting it get it. You can see the collision approaching in slow motion at the moment that a very musical minister arrives in a town not quite big enough for both of them; but you can see it too when a long-served fabric convener spots the arrival of an imaginative young architect in the midst of the congregation. For that matter, you can see the stress increase when the new minister announces she does not like flower vases on the communion table, where they have been since the beadle's mother who died last month first started putting them there in the very vases she gifted just after her wedding in 1955. You can see the anxiety in the eyes of the Deacons' Court clerk who realises in horror that the new Session Clerk is doing the Session minutes on a computer, and someone soon is surely going to want all minutes done the same way, far outside his area of competence.

It can happen to anyone; their insecurities are pressed, even in the very institution where they thought they should have safe space made for them, and sometimes, sadly, they do something to try to put right by force (because nothing else will work) what is making them feel so threatened.

Bullying

According to the law of the Church " 'bullying' shall mean any behaviour (including speech, writing or action, or any combination of them) which in the opinion of the Presbytery would alarm or distress a reasonable person or compel his or her actions or decisions unfairly". [Act IV 2007]

In every human institution, in every period of history, personal interaction suffers from the mildest versions of that human sin, so mild that most of the time people do not resort to legal process, so mild that most of the time people would not use the lexicon of 'bullying' language to describe it. In fact the legal use of it tends to be confined to two sorts of very unusual circumstances: first, when the alleged bully is thought to have dishonourable motives for their activity; and, second, when the bully is regarded as exercising great strength or authority that must be curbed. So the victims of other kinds of bullying are pressurised to disregard it through arguments like 'This says more about him than about you' and 'Don't lower yourself to her level' and 'He's only expressing a legitimate opinion you don't happen to share'. In each case those applying the pressure have not realised what a mischief there is to be acknowledged where the bullying has everything to do with weakness, not strength, and everything to do with wanting to achieve perfectly good ends, not evil ones.

When behaviour does not seem to warrant the use of an emotive word like 'bullying', it is all too easy to underestimate it. Low-level manipulation, skilful political operating, tactical 'dealing' in the commodities of status, task and respect; these run through congregational life, often amongst the sweetest, most dedicated, wisest and kindest of people, all trying to do the right thing and even for the right reasons. Spotting it is three-quarters of the battle in surviving it.

Strength and weakness

Weakness is a terribly underestimated threat in church life. It marks not only the causes and motivations for bullying behaviour, but it characterises the very conduct itself in ways that some ministers and office-bearers never seem to recognise, fascinating ways that explain why the worshipping community is always such a complicated social organism.

Strength is rarely the initial cause when one person uses distress or compulsion to bend another to his aims. If this individual were in a position of strength, with the better argument or the church's regulation or the majority of the Kirk Session on his side, there would be no need to waste bullying behaviour (and therefore reputation) on the situation, as the debate would be won before it had begun. Rather, it is the very person who fears their own fragility who jumps in despair over the line between acceptable and unacceptable personal dynamics, doing whatever it takes to protect something they fear losing.

When it comes to method, weakness is used as often as strength in the setting of the Church (where the weak are supposed to be so particularly welcome). In a show of his strength, the praise band leader who is defeated in a passionate Session debate tonight may be suddenly and mysteriously unavailable for next week's family service, wrecking a special occasion most effectively. In a show of her strength, the offended elder whose grand-daughter's baptism the minister was unable to agree to do may mobilise her friends on the Board to vote against the minister's pet buildings plan. In a gesture of utter weakness, though, the disappointed Sunday School teacher may burst uncontrollably into tears upon discovering that she's due to take the difficult P7 boys, and the terrified Superintendent opts for the easy life by re-shuffling the staff instead. That was bullying. In an apparent expression of weakness, a certain kind of church worker will adopt full martyr mode, doing jobs others admire them for doing, always with an air of selfless suffering, and milking the resulting sympathy for all its worth when times are hard. That is bullying.

Those who have worked out the possibilities of weakness as a lever might as well discover here in this book that the newest generation of Church of Scotland ministers has been taught to identify and disarm the very archetype of that tactic, the use of threatened resignation. One of the greatest fears of many ministers is the difficulty of recruiting people into certain posts (treasurer, safeguarding co-ordinator, property convener, and the like). Those who undertake those roles benefit from a background atmosphere of relieved gratitude, because by their presence they keep the spectre of an unfillable vacancy at bay. The biggest lever they have in any dispute – a dispute that may have nothing whatever to do with that job – is the threat that they will resign, and leave the minister, Session Clerk or other adversary with a nightmare of a hole.

Our probationers are advised to adopt a strategy that will cost short-term pain for a long-term prize worth the price. Always, always accept resignations, genuine or tactical. Never, ever reverse the decision. Accept them quickly, courteously, regretfully even, but unwaveringly. Do the job yourself for a time, if that's what it takes. If it happens a second time, the second person probably failed to understand what was happening, and it really, really will not happen a third time. Or perhaps it will, but it won't be for purposes of bullying; it will be the bullies giving up and going away.

Well-intentioned bullies

Another tendency of the fallen human condition is to imagine that one must be morally superior to one's rivals in an argument. Just as God must be on my side when my country is at war, so the most intense disagreements in congregational life can blind the combatants into thinking there is a battle of good and evil intentions taking place, and no-one ever believes he is on the 'wrong' side. Those outside the struggle can see both points of view with an impartial eye: Presbytery and Assembly Clerks trying to give procedural advice, staff members in the Ministries Council and elsewhere, ministers who might be lucky enough not to be embroiled in the argument, people in unconnected congregations, all can see the good but incompatible visions that divide people to the point of bitterness.

The fact that someone is indulging in improper behaviour to secure their own interests is no evidence that their interests are bad ones. The most sincerely-held beliefs can result in the most unfair behaviour. The most profoundly-sensed vocation can make people stop at nothing to secure a role of leadership. An unshakable belief about our faith's moral teachings can lead to hurtful opposition to another person's choices in life. Were not many of the Old Testament's prophets bullies, really, as they told out an unpalatable truth, most assuredly causing distress and alarm to perfectly reasonable people and unapologetically trying to compel their behaviour before it was too late for them?

The trouble is, it would be so much neater and easier, and so much more satisfying, if one's opponents could be guaranteed to be the bad guys. Yet even those whose bad judgement takes my breath away are doing their best for the Church that is theirs as much as mine, and for the God of both of us.

Disarming with trust

Those who are called to the highest tasks of leadership in the Church community have the task of preventing and removing the games of power they find around them. First and foremost they will long to avoid being players in those games themselves, but their own tasks and status conspire to place them directly in that harm's way from many directions.

Those who succeed best of all, so much so that they manage to continue to love their people and even to be loved in return, often include those who practise the extraordinary and noble discipline of attributing the best of motivations to everyone they encounter. Such a minister, who disagrees with a member on the most far-reaching question of moral principle, or contends with a colleague over an irksome detail of practice, nevertheless has it in her to treat the other as having a perfectly legitimate point of view and the right for it to be heard and weighed with respect. Friendship and love are bigger there than the anxieties that produced the disagreement. That minister, in fact, is probably more secure than most, and less driven by deep fragility within her own spirit.

How different the General Assembly or Presbytery would be if everyone there treated everyone else as being good and godly, even when believing their arguments to be wrong. How disarming of the few who are just too ruthless, when they are not given the satisfaction of an asymmetric fight against someone they can bend or compel.

Consider the awful responsibility of co-ordinating the appraisal and adjustment of parish resources. There now is a role and a task that is rarely coveted in any Presbytery. There is a convener who does not relish his status, and few struggle to keep the job. But there is someone with an infinite capacity to bring out the worst and most paranoid feelings in those he encounters in his work.

The hearts of members of the Church's Commission of Assembly, which hears appeals in adjustment cases, inevitably sink as the papers and pleadings arrive, revealing yet another argument by congregational members who have persuaded themselves that their Presbytery is out to get them, has it in for them, has always been trying to do them down, is taking wicked pleasure in closing them... and the reader will know of other familiar complaints. Those Commission members are themselves members of other Presbyteries, and know that no-one takes pleasure in the loss of a congregation, and know that it is with the heaviest of hearts that their committees find ways to meet the challenge of shrinking financial resources throughout Scotland, and know how painful it all is for sensitive, decent ministers and elders to have to make these things happen. If the complainers had attributed kindly motives to their Presbytery's representatives, they would be working with them to make the best of their circumstances, not heading towards the shock of being put out of their misery by the Commission.

The Golden Rule

There is a secret formula for all of this grief and tension. It is a formula as old as the Gospel that expresses it: do to others as you would have them do to you. Some rules are just too big to be achievable, because it would involve such a change of spirit to live life entirely like that, and few of us are ready for such total transformation. So we take the rule and apply it in little ways and convenient occasions; or we apply it to others and judge their conduct and not our own against it. We scorn the rule when we are admiring those who get what they want by being tough, though perhaps after all they get what they want by being weak bullies.

But perhaps congregational life, those few hours in the week when that human machine comes together to do its thing, perhaps that is a place just small enough for the Golden Rule to work. At every turning-point of discussion, at every moment of allocation of status or task, in every difficult encounter, things are turned upside down for good when one of the parties thinks into the place and need and point of view of the other, and asks what that person expects of him in exactly that moment. In our cinematic age, we can imagine turning the camera round to film each scene over the shoulder of the other person, our own faces being the focus of the drama, our choices being the substance of the plot. Entering the other person's needs, suspicions and fears breaks through to him more than any other approach.

What, for instance, would happen if every member of every church choir in Scotland recorded their own voice, singing along to a CD of hymns, and listened to it? What would happen if each of them pretended to be the local choirmaster, and asked 'Would we be better off if the choir did not include this voice?'. And what would happen if those who realised it was time for them to go invented an elegant excuse for leaving, so that the choirmaster would not be compelled to fib 'but you have a lovely voice' and find both of them back where they started?

What would happen if the members of large and wealthy congregations bit back the old argument 'you can't close us, we are financially self-sustaining' when the Presbytery was talking about uniting their 300 members with a congregation of 400 members lying 250 yards away, into their building that seats 800? What would happen if their Kirk Session took a few hours to go and visit the massively aid-receiving congregation of 50, which just happened to have a much higher *per capita* giving than theirs and lay 25 miles from the next church building of any kind, and thought a bit about all that?

What would happen if the elder who has read the lesson at the Watchnight Service for the last twenty years let go a little and tried to get inside the thinking of the Bible Class leader, who would love to ask one of her 12-year-olds to do that reading and have an experience of worship that could inspire him for a lifetime? Or better still, what would happen if that elder went one step further and congratulated the child on the reading, whether it was done well or badly?

Faith is ennobled and strengthened every week in parishes across the Church of Scotland, whenever the upside-downness of the Gospel gets the better of people.

Pen portrait

He felt the Church life that he had always known slipping out of his grasp during the ministry that had recently ended. Things had changed too much, too suddenly. Committee Conveners who had served faithfully for many years had been replaced with young men and women who brought written reports rather explaining everything carefully in the Session meeting. The minister seemed to spend a great deal of time with people outside the congregation, and not enough with his own flock. Agreeing to become the Session Clerk had seemed the right thing to do, to recover what was vanishing, somehow to hold the line and keep some of what was sacred. The invitation had come too late, though; things had gone too far to be righted.

The minister had been about his own age, but seemed quick to concede precious things to the Presbytery in the new linkage he had taken on mid-ministry. Co-operation on service times with the rural congregation, rationalisation of buildings, the loss of the manse, things like these had to be done of course. Why, though, did the larger congregation have to give up its Watchnight Service? That was the centre-point of the town's Christmas celebration for as long as anyone could remember, the time the whole community came together for worship regardless of anyone's beliefs. The Session Clerk always read the passage about the shepherds and angels, and surely that was a fitting task. That service, surely, should not have gone. The country congregation could have managed without it; it was managing now without the mid-morning service on Remembrance Sunday, after all.

There was a bright glimmer of hope on the horizon, in the form of a 25 year old probationer whose name had emerged from the Nominating Committee processes, and who seemed likely to become the new minister. This would be his first charge, and he would have everything to learn. He would be glad of the guiding influence of an older Session Clerk, someone who knew the area, someone who knew what people here liked to see done, someone who knew the score on many things.

There was quite a lot that could be done quickly by a Clerk to make the new lad settle in to a successful and acceptable ministry. It would be no trouble to take over completely the preparation of the agendas of future Session meetings, ensuring continuity with the past. It would be helpful to produce an initial list of pastoral visits. And it would be very useful to have dinner together in the first couple of weeks, so that the minister could hear something impartial about each of the office-bearers and elders, to know which were positive thinkers, which understood the culture of the place, and which were risky newcomers with strange ideas belonging to their previous congregations.

It would need only some fast, firm action by the minister as soon as he was inducted, to re-establish the Watchnight Service – six months away still, so no harm could possibly be done...

Worship, spirituality and entertainment

The tour guide was no more than 22, obviously a student working to pay his way through college, and there was nothing out of the ordinary about him. In such a poor country he had that slightly wistful pride in the best of the culture, the things tourists had to see as if it was terribly important. The bus reached some especially significant Orthodox church amongst the hundreds in that region, and the tourists shuffled in looking around, looking for what was to take their attention, looking at the strangeness of it compared with the parish church back home. The guide instinctively blessed himself, moved to one of the icons, kissed it, stood there for the length of a silent prayer, and continued his patter as if nothing had happened. His charges – the ones who were not Roman Catholic – envied him for just a moment, tried to imagine their own young adult children pausing in respectful worship with such natural ease.

The Catholics in the group could make something of their visit. From their internal library each of them could summon reliable pieces of writing, prayers taught to them so long ago they had spoken or mumbled or silently uttered them thousands of times. They had words that were right when they gazed up into the majestic dome and saw for a moment the glory of the Father. They had words that were right when they looked at the sadness of the Virgin's face in an icon reminding them of the Passion. They had words that were right when they came face to face with the baby Jesus holding his arm in blessing, and felt a gush of tenderness towards his humanity.

The Protestants in the group waited to be told about it all. Some of them ran through the Lord's Prayer in their minds, and that was about it really.

It would be a brave and pushy minister who asked the members of their congregation whether and how they prayed and worshipped God in private. How many answers would they receive? Some would tell them that is none of their business, minister or not. Some would argue that is what ministers are there to do, and people who go to church a lot, and not a job for ordinary people. Some would say they would not presume to do it, and don't have such a high conceit of their own religion. And some would admit they do not know what they should do, what they should say, how long they should go on, what they could include, whether they can say what they think. And some would confess they are afraid to try, and some would blurt out that the thought of something so intimate embarrasses them. And most, when pressed, would say no-one has ever told them what to do.

And some would say they prayed, but their prayers would entirely be prayers for others, a list of names of family and loved ones, with the occasional addition of someone in particular distress, someone for whom prayers were promised. There would though be no wrestling with demons or conscience, no weeping over the frustrations of life, no pouring out of anger or bitterness, no railing against ill-treatment in relationships or injustice in daily work, no struggling to overcome terrible guilt and break through to new beginnings, no reluctant realisation of a completely new direction in which to walk or work or worship. Most, you see, would tell you no-one has ever told them what to do.

Sunday by Sunday many of them go to their church to do all the things they do not do day by day. Somehow, in the company of dozens of people with different lives, different families, different pressures and different griefs, they must turn their own lives, families, pressures and griefs over in their hearts, dare to ask what their feelings long to ask, disentangle the knots they know God will see more simply, and find peace from whatever torments them. With 168 hours in the week when they might have taken the chance to feel themselves alone with God to concentrate on their own souls, they have waited until everyone is gathered together because they do not know how to pray and worship alone. They turn their minds to the One who loves them more than anyone has loved them, but only in a crowd where the words are the words of a group, shared words, words in common. They are not the unique words of a man who this week has survived something no-one else in church could understand, or done something so unforgettable that his spirit alone is darkened by it. So they worship to the extent that they can do so in common with everybody else around them; but they never worship alone and never address what is most personal and individual.

What tremendous responsibility lies upon those who decide what will fill the Sunday hour of public prayer. They will be to blame if those in their pastoral care are left with terrible and wonderful things unspoken before God in that hour and in their daily lives. They will be to blame if nothing echoes in the souls of the faithful. And so they will be to blame whenever an act of worship is not actually an act of worship, for then the people's need will be left entirely unmet.

They, the ministers and preachers of the Church, are to blame when the Sunday service becomes an exercise in entertainment and enticement in the face of the competition surrounding the life of the Church. No doubt the sheer amount of competition presses in on the Church in a way unknown to a previous generation, for in our generation honesty has broken out and there remains almost no pretence in our secular culture that space should be left for Christian worship and Sabbath peace. Little girls are torn between Sunday School and Pony Club. Little boys find football practice takes place at 11 o'clock each term-time Sunday. Adults with working weeks of 70 hours need time at home in the quietness Sunday morning offers. Much of the competition harming the Church comes in the form of slick and professional entertainment that far exceeds anything the local congregation can muster. Few Church choirs would produce anything a 15-year-old would prefer to the content of her MP3 player. Few sermons would be as attractive to a young adult as twenty minutes surfing the net. Most Church interiors cannot compete with the virtual worlds of electronic gaming. The Church is foolish to try to compete directly in a battle where she does not stand a chance of winning. When she tries, she steps into the world of entertainment and loses her soul.

Inch by inch, hymn by hymn, a Sunday morning ecclesiastical entertainment can push aside real worship, push aside the chance for men, women and children to encounter the sense of the presence of God and the sense of being able to ponder the most unexpected and irregular and unique and personal things. When the performance of the music - or let's face it when the performers of the music – are the object of attention, where is worship? When the children's address is memorable only for its cookery lesson or conjuring trick or witty punch-line or revelation about life in the manse, do these little ones learn to toddle towards God somehow? When it is the substance of the preaching and not the language that is simple, and the great tangle of each person's home and work and passions and problems and fears and tentative hopes are bypassed by a message that does not begin to touch any of them, can those who hear the thin words truly bring everything to God and feel entirely known by Him?

All the preachers need to do – the phrase is intentionally ironic in tone – all they need to do is offer what the slick, smooth world of entertainment will never provide: the practice of the presence of God, a glimpse of the divine, an experience of the holy. Discharging that terrible responsibility, to express other people's worship and find the words to represent their innermost needs and feelings, is the hardest challenge for every minister. Finding words that can be rightly addressed to God stretches the spiritual resources of everyone who composes public prayer. The man or woman who voices the praises and sorrows and intercessions of others exposes with utter transparency their own relationship with God. When that relationship sounds shallow and disappointing to someone in the congregation, the minister has failed that worshipper, failed to deepen an encounter with the divine, failed to develop that member's devotion and faith.

One kind of preacher constantly tells God things He certainly already knows, most commonly what a lovely day it is today as we gather for worship. There is nothing anyone could say in prayer that is not already known to the Father, true; but this small-talk cannot possibly be appropriate. Often, too, God appears to be treated as requiring instruction. Prayers of thanksgiving become rather like cheerful news bulletins, full of items both the congregation and the Almighty already know perfectly well. If God is particularly unfortunate, this leader will go beyond mere fact and preach a little sermon, handing up orders for what is expected in the week to come. The intelligent worshipper who had come to church with an open heart, willing to think about something in a new way, is at best bored, at worst irritated, and certainly not improved or intrigued or provoked or changed in the slightest.

Another type of minister declines to address God directly at all, or only so apologetically that contact seems scarcely to have been attempted let alone achieved. This may come about by the unfailing use of the Ecclesiastical Subjunctive, a little-studied but widespread grammatical offence in which prayer is always expressed as if conditionally. We would praise you; we would ask for ...; we would bring X in prayer. Would you? When would you? Won't you? Why don't you get on with it then? Or it may 'just' be done the other way. We just want to praise you; we just ask; or even (combining both techniques) we would just pray for X. What, only just? Is nothing more merited? Are you praying merely? Do you have no boldness, no ambition? The Church member who is resolved to deepen his own prayers, who truly has the rare courage to try to come closer to his God, will be left empty by the kind of public worship cursed by false modesty, that seems to avoid frankness at all costs and with every word.

Two more ministers each miss the ears of their congregation with words too high or too low. The first has read somewhere that it matters terribly that preaching should not be shallow or empty, and he has mistaken depth for sophistication. His theological lectures have a rhetorical construction (and length) of which Cicero would be proud, and few corners of postmodernist thought are left unexplored. Quotations, liberally scattered through the text, come from books he is confident few of the congregation have read. The congregation, each feeling a little like Winnie the Pooh stuck in Rabbit's front door and having improving books read to one end of him by Christopher Robin, suspect this must be good for them and greatly admire the minister's learning. But one lady can see no connection between anything she hears and her inability to sleep since her husband went to Kandahar with the RAF. One man turns over in his mind the affair that ended his marriage and does not know how to find peace, and his thoughts are never broken into by the wash of sound coming from the direction of the pulpit. One younger adult wonders what the minister would say to the character in Eastenders who has just discovered she has cancer, and decides it would probably be too hard to understand.

The second minister, who has sat through a few of the other's sermons before she was herself ordained last year, has read somewhere that it matters terribly that preaching should not be inaccessible to ordinary people, and has mistaken clarity for simplicity. Her virtually-identical sermons stress how easily every part of life will fall sweetly into place once a commitment has been made to a few religious propositions, how complete will be the sense of forgiveness, how quickly fears will be relieved, and how pleasant it will be to live a life blessed by God with the extra blessing only believers can expect. One Sunday some familiar visitors arrive from her former congregation. The lady who cannot sleep, the pilot's wife, now begins to wonder whether her faith is inadequate and blameworthy, for she knows she will no more sleep tonight than any other night. The divorced man wishes it were so simple to assume that God forgives him and move on, but suspects there are others whose forgiveness he may also need before the knot in his stomach untangles. The Eastenders fan imagines his favourite character here this morning, and decides she would just feel angry.

Another minister pretends to address God and uses the opportunity to preach at the people without admitting to it. Intercessions become social comment, while supplication is replaced by arbitrary moralising. This is particularly noticeable to the trained ear at the beginning of difficult, tense court and committee meetings in the Church, where the person chairing the business opens with a prayer which leaves everyone present in no doubt what the correct outcome of the deliberations should be. When the Congregational Board is on the verge of ordering expensive buildings works the minister hoped to avoid, and he prays at length about the financial needs of the World Church, he is abusing his place. The genuinely pious member will feel that God is being ignored, treated as if He was not listening, treated as if we had nothing to say for the Divine to hear; and that feeling comes on top of the infuriating feeling of being manipulated in a vulnerable moment.

Another minister is afraid to talk about difficult things, and certainly afraid to preach on passages in the Bible that deal with hard subjects like death and failure and sex and doubt and loneliness. The Gospels and a few selected passages in Old Testament history provide a safe diet of morality tales and warm re-assurance of God's approval of nice moral people. The lectionary is roundly avoided, along with half the books of the Bible. The dirty, scary things are left at the church door as people come in, much as they are left at the door of the bowling club and the evening class. They can be picked up again at the beginning of the new week, but they are not nice enough to bring up in church. The struggler and sufferer whose life frightens them goes away from church with their fears intact.

Another minister manages to reach the opposite extreme somehow; and far from asking too little in worship raises expectations to incredible heights. Irrational demands for incredible and unreasonable stunts on God's part take the breath away. Orders are put in for particular weather at a particular time, usually for particular local function and rarely for drought-stricken countries in general, oddly enough. People of faith are expected to bypass the NHS and achieve a speed of recovery for which there is no discernable good reason. Those attending are required to find the experience spectacular and supernatural in every regard, or else they are not real believers at all. The genuinely reflective worshipper feels uncomfortable that God is being asked for magic tricks, and is not prepared to behave that way in his own life of prayer.

Sometimes the most poignant omission of all is a minister's avoidance of lamentation in worship. If most of the population do not regard themselves as part of the Church, it may be largely because most of the population have fears and griefs for which there is no trite remedy, but they are faced by a Church that is too often too cheery. In these days when horrible problems remain unresolved despite everything, an only-triumphant Church does not give space and time to those who know in the core of their soul that they have not won through. A Church whose praise band can play any triumphant psalm six times without stopping, and even sits down by the rivers of Babylon with a happy catchy tune, may never allow anyone to use the rest of the Psalter to shout at God, demand an answer, weep. Offering silence, when too many would offer a shallow answer, can make a safe space for an angry spirit who needs to be met in the worst of the storm and not only when all is calm and bright.

There are leaders in the Church who are big enough and strong enough to do the one thing that is needful, to enable the worship of God by those in their care and to open the way for men, women and children to be honest in their depths. Like children approaching Jesus without fear, they say what they know is on their people's minds and say it to God without evasion or circumlocution or pretended apology. They use words that all can hear and comprehend, but they give their hearers ideas they have never before thought. They pose questions without knowing what the answers must be, and speak in joy and sorrow with equal candour. They pray as if they know they might be changed by it, but never as if they think they will change God.

If they are as fortunate and thoughtful as this, men and women longing to do the right thing will find the worship of their congregation has a structure and order that can bear the weight of everything the human soul needs to pour into their devotion to God. Their public worship provides the shape for their private prayer and thought, and the pattern and substance of the Sunday service sustains the reflection and spirituality of the coming week. It is adequate for complicated lives, and gives permission to leave none of the complexity behind when the soul presents itself in private prayer. These people can bring themselves to a sense of the presence of God, as if in their imaginations they have approached some special place or moment. In their minds they know that God will be in every instant as close to them as their own breathing; but in their hearts they know too that their humanity prevents them from remembering that without a special effort, a special remembrance, and so that special place, special moment. They can use the language they have heard in church to try to adore God who they know is beyond all language, but they know it is still worth trying. They learn the discipline of setting aside for a moment their flawed self-centredness, and contemplate something far beyond their own condition. They can ponder their own greatest needs and regrets, confessing what is wrong and looking at themselves courageously. They can confidently ask for the forgiveness and empowerment that promises the lost need not stay lost, and not feel they are conceited or presumptuous in doing so. They can probably forgive themselves when their mental health would otherwise fail under some burden of guilt too heavy to carry through ordinary living. They can summon up the courage to consider their onward journey, and to discover possibilities they had not found in any other place. Unexpected opportunities may open because there is faith enough to entertain the challenges, and humility enough to acknowledge God-given talent. They can rejoice in the goodness of other people's lives without envy, mourn what hurts in another with sincerely shared pain, and ask for blessing of them without prescription and direction.

Or as the kind of parish minister who makes the Church a good place said to a school service many years ago: say thank you, say sorry, say please.

Into their hands people will entrust the most intimate spiritual exercises. The new widow who comes to the 'Blue Christmas' service early in Advent, to spend an hour in quiet contemplation because the Nativity Play and Watchnight Service would crush her this year, is able to worship in her raw state. The couple standing stricken by the new grave of their soldier son on a windless November morning will find presence in two minutes' silence and live on the strength of it until next year, though they do not know how. That soldier's mates, with heads bowed at the Drumhead ceremony in Camp Bastion, will listen with painful intensity to a padre whom they would not expect to see smile during it. A pregnant woman who could not be more happy or excited, but feels the enormity of the challenge of motherhood ahead, may have some very direct petitions to make to God, and really needs to be able to do so without pussyfooting about as if her prayer were an unfortunate imposition that wastes Heaven's time. A teenager soon to leave home has many decisions to make about the style of life to choose, and whether to go all out for personal success or to dedicate time and emotion to other people; and so he needs to have a conscience that is alive and challenged.

None of these people needs to be an intellectual. All they need, all they want, is for the experience of life to include the experience of spiritual life.

Are our services acts of worship?

Pen Portrait

Thank you, Father Joe, for asking me to say a few words about my visit to the Parish Church last week. We've often shared ecumenical services, where there were bits of different traditions, and nobody really thought it was a normal service for them. So this is a great idea, to send a different member of the congregation to a different local church each week, to find out what they normally do.

I think I was most struck by what Church of Scotland people don't do, and it left me feeling a bit uncertain. To start with they don't seem to bless themselves. There was no holy water when I went in, so it felt a bit funny. They don't show any reverence for their altars, but I don't think they even call them altars. Certainly the whole service came and went and the only thing they put there was the offering baskets. Of course there was no Mass, and I knew there wouldn't be, but everything else seemed to be stretched out to fill the space, and the service only lasted 55 minutes. The oddest thing was the congregation's part in the service, or rather the lack of it. They didn't leave their pews at any point (and I'm told if they were having communion they still wouldn't); and apart from the Lord's Prayer they didn't say anything either. You just to do a lot of listening in that Church.

I was struck by the minister. I've always thought we gave more respect to you, Father, than Protestants like to give to their clergy. Well I know their ministers can't just decide everything for themselves, because they have those elders who have to have meetings about things. So I was surprised just how much of a one-man show it was. I suppose that was partly because they don't have anything like servers, so the minister spends the whole service all on his own at the front. I think it was partly because he did almost everything himself. There was a woman who got up to read an Epistle lesson, but apart from that it was all just the one voice. And then of course he spoke longer than you normally do, Father; but that was OK because it gave quite a bit of time to think about what he was saying and decide whether I agreed with all of it.

The biggest question I took there was whether I'd feel as if it would be a religion that was different to mine. It wasn't at all. There were things we do here, and things we say, that don't appear in their service at all. But there was nothing in their service that I had a problem with. Well, just the things they *didn't* do!

A Church Without Walls

The General Assembly of 1999 got into one of those fankles that the General Assembly never admits it has. The perennial debate about executive authority between Assemblies, and about the existence of the constantly-morphing Assembly Council, brought out the most contentious instincts in the leading characters of that year. There seemed to be a choice before the Assembly: to change the clothes of the Council once again, or to pause for a year or two and undertake a deeper study of questions about review and reform of the Church, a Church which always remembers the Reforming motto *semper reformanda* (always in need of being reformed).

It never ceases to amaze those who serve the Assembly at close quarters that such a large and cumbersome body has the ability to come to such elegant and intelligent solutions to knotty problems faced by the Church's administration. It is rare for the Assembly to achieve an outcome that seems ugly and unnecessary. The General Assembly of 1999 probably did so though, when it decided both to reform the existing institution a little further and to set up a Special Commission to look at those underlying questions. Probably it wasted thousands of hours of some people's time, and it is to be hoped they will never realise who they were. And yet, in the Special Commission itself, an amazing phenomenon produced more changes in congregational life than any other single Report of the decade.

The Commission in the course of its two years of deliberations wrestled over the curious question whether Presbyterianism could be described as institutionalised distrust, but perhaps they were tempted by that conclusion only when they were most tired. The 1999 Assembly, for all its faults, illustrated that Presbyterianism at its best is institutionalised trust, when it appointed a 'Special Commission anent Review and Reform in the Church' with its membership having an average age below 40, and its Convener being Peter Neilson. Along with unmistakable spiritual strength and confidence, Peter brought two key qualities to his task. First, he is one of a tiny number of ministers who are trusted across the theological breadth of the Church. There are quite a few individuals who are *respected* across that diversity of points of view, whose personal integrity and piety are recognised and admired; but far fewer who are actually *trusted*, allowed to exercise a leadership that is acknowledged and followed so widely. Second, Peter can talk the language of management and organisational theory, and can translate the structures and needs of the Church into that language, so that the Commission was able to say things that resonated with those who yearned for the Church to do things better, but also with those deeply suspicious of the language of business in the Body of Christ.

For two years the hugely disparate group encountered each other, befriended each other, allowed themselves to be spiritually developed and encouraged by Peter, and wrestled with the most frustrating, challenging and exciting questions about the Church's mission. Daring honesty was expressed, sacred cows were questioned, and completely different ways of living out the Church's life were explored. The more complicated the task before them became, the more the group felt the desire to bring the simplest possible Report, literally a two-word quote from Jesus: 'follow me' – with everything else the Commission needed to say contained in a large Appendix. They resisted the temptation.

The 'Church Without Walls' Report

The Special Commission brought its final report – by now known as 'Church Without Walls' – to the Assembly of 2001. It has generated huge initiatives in every layer of the Church's structures, producing a generational change for the whole institution. Even those ministers and congregations who were not inclined to engage with it directly have been affected for good by its results, and most are involved with its indirect effects, some of them without realising it.

Centrally, that process of reconfiguration of the Assembly Council continued until 2005, when the Church exercised corporate trust to a new extent and established the current Council of Assembly with an executive co-ordinating authority that had always been dangerously absent between Assembly weeks. The proper tension between effectiveness (in governance, finance, staffing and administration) and constant reform (through new ideas and timeless challenges) is maintained in the life of the Assembly and throughout the year. Even disagreement has been creative and productive, as when subsequent Special Commissions (one on Structure and Change and another on the Third Article Declaratory) examined the Council of Assembly's critique of parts of the Church Without Walls Report's findings on the national roles of the Church of Scotland, and used that to produce further reform.

Regionally, a struggle for reform of Presbyteries has been waged throughout the decade since the Report was received by the Church. The Special Commission was not the kind of body to achieve the transformation it knew was needed, and others (most recently the Panel on Review and Reform) have wrestled with new ideas and old resistances. There are fiefdoms to be dismantled. There are interests invested in the current crazy disparity in Presbytery sizes: when Presbyteries, unit by unit, play their constitutional part in the approval of major legislative change, two tiny Presbyteries outvote one massive one (and on current theological spread around Scotland this gives one end of the theological spectrum a disproportionate power). A great deal of self-interest stands in the path of regional reform.

Congregational life, though, was the central focus of the Commission's work. The Report confirmed the understanding of the Church that the national and regional structures exist to serve the local Church, which exists largely still in the form of congregations. Transparency has become one hallmark of the changes: Kirk Sessions now meet openly, as Presbyteries had always done, and committees and Councils all over the Church publish their minutes. Simplicity is another hallmark: dozens of congregations every year escape from the tortuous separation of apparently 'spiritual' and apparently 'temporal' decisions, transferring to the Unitary Constitution, leaving everything to the authority of the Kirk Session, and allowing the engagement of individual talents and passions in a structure of groups and appointments suited in every congregation to its exact needs and resources. The third hallmark has been celebration: gatherings, seminars, exhibitions and rallies have punctuated the Church's life ever since 2001, attracting many people's enthusiasm and leaving many others utterly uninspired and cheerfully unengaged, but that is the breadth and glory of the Church.

It was a single principle, more than any structural suggestion or sequence of events, that was the genius of the Report, and represents the most difficult thing the Church can try to bring to life. 'A Church Without Walls' asks all of us to remove walls, and things like walls, in our church lives, to resist the temptation to be a community apart from community, a world separate from the world. In a Reformed Church that did not retain the tradition of enclosed monastic life, the principle demands that the whole Church does not allow itself to be one great separate group.

The principle badly needs to be broadcast. In one parish after another, the effort of ministers and people is designed to persuade local people to walk through the door of a building and attend something that is happening there for them. It may be a service or an meeting of some kind, it may be an explicitly religious event or a social activity, it may be designed to attract new people or be part of the routine of existing members; but it requires a person to come from outside into the inside, to step over a threshold – through a wall – that will not be an insignificant or invisible line to them. That is a Church defined by walls.

A dying congregation, whose membership is currently in denial and whose epitaph will be written in only a few years, proudly announces on its beautiful notice board that local people can come inside and get together for coffee and chat. The local population do nothing of the kind. They have no reason whatsoever to make the time to do so, have no idea who will be there already, do not need any more friends than they have, and would need to know what the chat was about anyway. On the local bus they pass the lovely building, and are probably delighted that something so pretty sits there in the middle of their community, especially if they might want to be married there, or need it for a particularly large funeral. But why on earth would anyone open that door, walk through it, and drink coffee and chat? The people who put the notice up really thought they were doing something new and attractive; but they have no difficulty crossing that threshold, for they have been doing it for years and know who else is in there with them.

Twenty miles away, an infamously enterprising minister (and former member of the Special Commission) spotted the newly-vacated Woolworth shop in the town his parish serves. Faster than it would take to think of reasons not to do it, he had a plan to take it over during Advent and make it part of the life of the town for a few weeks, benefiting the Church but rubbing out any imagined boundary-line between the congregation and the wider community. The community was involved, nowhere near the Church's own walls.

There are, of course, church walls people love to enter. The national Church is guardian, for good or ill, of much of the built heritage of Scotland, and thousands of people from around the world and down the road are delighted to cross the threshold and wonder at the meaning of the stones and glass. In a distinctively Scottish way, our denomination is translating into its own practices the best of the 'cathedral tradition' in England, the phenomenon by which church growth bucks the more general trend of decline in the great historic places of ceremonial, expert musicianship, ancient art and continuity of familiar worship. The point is that people come to those spaces because they are the very special spaces they are, not because they are *our* spaces where we invite, require, chivvy people to come onto our territory. Too often the majesty of the space is removed and replaced with bits of paper, notice-boards, electronic displays, TV screens, all proudly narrating the churchy busy-ness of people who behave as if they own the place. They stomp all over the magic of the place, and take away its peace, the relief its quietness will bring to noisy souls who might be fortunate enough to find it just when they need it. So the Church, even where it has the most beautiful buildings, has to be a Church without walls by letting anyone permeate those walls, coming in and going out, without pressure and without clutter.

And people do, in their hundreds of thousands, at Watchnight. They come for reasons it would be impertinent and condescending to analyse. Those reasons may have to do with memories of something that was taught to people as precious and never entirely lost, something they need to touch on that magic day. Those reasons probably include the things that are happening on that occasion: resonant music, familiar words, the anonymity of darkness and a crowd, the luminal mystery of the midnight hour. Those reasons, surely, surely have absolutely nothing to do with the regular congregation inviting the others to come and join them in their space on that day at that hour. The Church need only make the slightest intimation that the service is taking place – or in most places just do nothing to suggest that it won't – and the people materialise with very clear expectations, in numbers so large that they have the confidence to do something they would not do alone.

That is a bonus, to have people permeating the walls from outside. The real question is whether the members of congregations really succeed in breeching the walls from within, to reach the world with the doing of good things and the telling of good words and the manifesting of good promises. Yet another Special Commission (you can tell something niggles the Church if several Commissions address similar questions in close succession) examined the national Church's responsibility to provide the ordinances of religion to Scotland as a whole. Overwhelmingly it discovered that Scottish institutions, significant individual leaders, and those in the very machinery of public service, still expect the Church of Scotland to provide its distinctive ministry throughout the communities of this country. Scotland may be more diverse than secular; or if she is secular she somehow does not deny a spiritual need.

One more product of the Church Without Walls process has enabled imaginative congregations to move their energy into their surrounding community: the Parish Development Fund. The fund provides grants and support to community projects that do not form part of the normal expenditure of a congregation. Where a congregation has been prompted by a social or pastoral need in its area and feels able to establish some way of helping there, it can use the untapped resources in its buildings, people and expertise, and provide something new. The Fund normally offers match-funding of some kind, requiring other funders to be involved. Other funders normally require there to be a benefit far beyond the membership of the congregation itself, beyond the worshipping life of the central group. The congregation is compelled to act without (or better still, to use a Scots word) outwith their walls.

Inner Walls

That, however, is about physical spaces, all of it. The Church, with or without its defining walls, is the place where I and millions like me confess a most terrifying truth; that though my body is filled with physical stuff, bones, muscles, organs, blood – filled right up tight so no spaces would be found if an anatomist were to cut me open – yet when I look in to myself I feel as if there is space there, huge space in which my mind moves about and my fears shiver and my passions pull me about, space enough to meet other people and to meet God whatever God may look like. That space, invisible and almost indescribable, is the most sacred of all. The Church has permission to occupy it, and must do so with an infinitely tender sensitivity. The Church has the responsibility to talk about it, and must do so with the most carefully-chosen words. It is what a contemporary church leader calls the middle of your middle, and it is a fearful thing to become aware of it. This too suffers from the building of walls, the keeping out or keeping in of the spirit, the posing of boundaries that should not be there.

Shibboleths of many kinds are used to establish who is inside the boundary and who remains an outsider. In one part of the Church, bald propositions of personal faith are posed for assent, rejecting any possibility that people find the claims of the Gospel complex, intriguing, mysterious. There is expected of them a brutal 'yes' as if to a closed question of some kind, but with that assent they are welcomed as if they have made in an instant the whole length of the journey from evil to good, from reprobate to saved, from beyond to within. Their personal spiritual space belongs safely inside a clearly-defined wall. In another part of the Church, particular habits of worship are demanded as an irreducible norm, as if the artistic tastes of those who maintain those patterns are an archetype given by God. Those who can manage to love those practices (and they may be anything from mass settings to praise bands, from silence to Victorian organ-music) are regarded as acceptable, and there is no moral duty to try to make sense for other people whose ears are just differently wired. The former group have an aesthetic sense that secures them within someone's wall. In yet another part of the Church an intellectual preacher is mismatched to a parish that has the temerity to be full of ordinary people, and casts around it a barrier of language that excludes most of the population. The minister, obviously, has not grasped the difference between intelligent preaching and intellectual preaching, and enjoys the latter far too much. A small coterie adore the stimulus; while the great majority discover that there is too great a distance to drive conveniently on a snowy Sunday morning to hear the neighbouring minister talk proper English. The space around which a wall is keeping them out is a mental space, and no-one should have the right to keep them out as if from a beautiful garden.

That is all perfectly lovely and extremely comfortable for the individuals who have enough good taste to step within the boundaries that are put in front of them, who decide to enter the magic circle that is offered to them. The vast majority who do not are left untouched by the Church, as if they deserved to be ignored now for not being attracted by the narrow offering extended to them in the first place. The real wickedness of it lies in the laziness permitted in those who place those invisible walls where they find them easiest to maintain for themselves: laziness because they are not breaking down the walls, moving across those boundaries and bringing love, care and service to those waiting outside.

There are just too many people who give the lie to that lazy way. There are just too many lovely people who make the world a better place but who do not have a sense of belonging securely and confidently in some part of the spectrum of the Church. There are just too many people who barely make it through the threshold of the Church, who sit – figuratively or literally – close to the door for an easy escape, and who patently live loving, sacrificial, outward-facing lives beyond the Church door. The shy beadle, who does far more than she is paid to do but does not believe that she could possibly become a member of an important organisation like the Church, because it is for better than the likes of her, is acting heroically every time she steps inside her work-place. The single parent bringing her child to the after-school club and loving it, but lacking the courage to come to Church at the weekend and sit alone without the excuse of her child to strengthen her, is troubled by the walls. The frail old gentleman who relishes the Afternoon Club in the Church hall once a week, where not only will he have tea and cakes but also a wee sing of a Moody and Sankey hymn remembered from his youth, has found the Church comes through its own walls to the place where he lives.

Chaplains Without Walls

In one large and growing area of the Church's ministry, working without and outwith walls has always been normal. Chaplaincies are spreading through more and more of society's institutions, defying the secularising narrative and creating touching-points between the Gospel and everyday life. In hospitals, prisons, the Armed Forces, industry, commerce and every kind of place of education, chaplains find themselves cast into someone else's world with the challenge of making it as naturally their own world as if they were in a comfortable familiar building, the kind with funny glass and strange furniture. They are thrown into situations full of people the Church would not otherwise meet or serve, and they have to live on their wits, bereft of the equipment and sacred space other ministers take for granted.

The institutional Church feels nervous, sometimes, because modern employment law has forced a shift for chaplains, away from the total control of their religious institution and into the secular employment of the place where they serve. NHS chaplains employed by the local trust, prison chaplains employed by the Scottish Prison Service; these and others lack another wall, a wall of institutional protection around them, keeping them to the tasks their Churches would like them to be doing, and exposed instead to their new world and its demands. They have to be trusted massively by the denominations that have sent them, trusted to keep faith with the fundamentals of their calling, trusted to exercise a recognisable ministry far beyond all sorts of ecclesiastical walls. The trust too comes from the receiving institution, the school or hospice or military establishment or oil company; these places welcome chaplains who have been sent their way with such freedom and responsibility.

There are, of course, other tempting walls to be found when they have arrived. The chaplain is quickly gathered into the walls of the institution in which she is meant to minister, learning its codes, following its routines, obeying its timetables, implementing its protocols, finding her place in its structures of authority and leadership. She discovers all over again the same dynamics of personal interaction, political intrigue, and good and evil, that she knew when she was sheltered inside the Church. She may be tempted to remain within these new walls, literal ones that hide her in a small space marked 'Chaplaincy', or the more important ones inside her head, that limit what she believes she can do and who she believes really needs her time and attention. Perhaps she will be the person who breaks down the needless walls of her new environment and does it a service it did not expect from her. Perhaps her own invisible walls of self-doubt and limited vision will be destroyed by the new possibilities she sees, to do things she has never seen the Church able to do before.

Bursting Walls

From time to time in the Church's history, some bursting out of energy has marked a terrifying and uncertain time, a time on which we look back with gratitude and a sense of the world transformed. The first Apostles, breaking out of their lives to set fire to the whole known world; the adventurer saints in the Middle Ages, taking possession of whole new countries in Northern Europe for the cause of Christ; the orders of friars, bringing fresh life to the preaching of the Gospel for ordinary people; the Reformers, Protestant and Catholic, re-connecting the Church with the biggest claims of the Gospel: every one of those movements broke down boundaries and barriers, limits and limitations. World-changers in those eras invaded society around them, and took away the excuse people had – the excuse we too often still give them by hiding from them – for ignoring what the Church is about and what the Church has to say.

Today, as we hardly dare to count the number of people who say they belong within our walls, we have learned – perhaps in the nick of time – that this is a foolish number to rely on. The elusive measure of our social capital should matter more to us, though it hardly suits journalists and critics who like a finite number and ideally a plummeting one. Today, as more and more often Churches draw an imaginary ring around particular articles of faith and then count the people who are able to assent to those articles, who feel they are standing within that ring, we have to learn anew that there are far more people who stand further out from the centre of our beliefs, gladly within earshot of the Gospel and earnestly living with all the integrity and purity they can manage. Today, as church buildings all over the country are refurbished to make them more like other places where people feel comfortable, we are dimly grasping that there is another way to serve other people's lives and make the whole world a more wholesome, holy place.

Pen Portrait

Ann sat in the car, very puzzled. The minister had not left his vestry yet, and the light there was still on. That conversation had not gone as she had expected at all.

Throughout her childhood she had been familiar with this parish Church, the place the school had come at Christmas and Easter. She knew its hall from Brownie days, and she'd been to funerals and weddings here from time to time. It was Church of Scotland, which meant it was the church that looked after everybody, didn't it? You would certainly think it belonged to the whole community, the way the minister took the Remembrance service at the war memorial every year, and served on the fund-raising committee at the High School, and had that column in the paper.

So when Ann and David had been living together for two years and decided they would get married and think about having a family, she had really looked forward to having the wedding in a building that meant so much to her family and where everything would look so lovely. She tried to do everything properly, and made the appointment to see the minister this evening before she booked anything else – before she booked the County Hotel, and that was a risk to leave very much longer if she was to get it on a Saturday in July next year.

The minister had got no further than asking for their addresses, and when he saw they lived together said he wouldn't be marrying them. He said something about Christian ideals of marriage, and the proper place of sex, and some policy by his Kirk Session, and the interview just stopped right there. What on earth was that about? Ann had never heard of that happening to anyone else before.

And at that moment two things made sense to her. The first one was the wedding schedule she'd signed as Joss's bridesmaid here last year. She couldn't quite figure why Joss's address on that form was shown as her parents' house, when she'd moved in with Derek long before then. No wonder; Joss had known something Ann wished she'd known about half an hour ago. Ann remembered Joss's wedding dress, and how well she'd disguised her pregnancy then. Well, well, and what did our minister make of that when he found out? And the second memory that flashed through her mind was Kate's wedding, actually not long after Joss's. That time Ann had wondered why that wedding took place in John's parents' church 50 miles away. No wonder again.

So that would be Plan B, presumably. Tell Dave what's happened, speak to his mum, and see what her minister will say. A bus would be able to bring the guests back to the County Hotel for the meal. The park would be fine for photos. As for coming along here on Sunday morning, on any Sunday morning...

Command, Leadership and Management

Every Church of Scotland congregation is a complex organism with several tasks to perform and a community to perform them. Learning the life of a congregation means encountering its people in different activities and in different groups. The community forms in some shape for some event – a service, a Sunday School session, a Guild meeting, a gardening group, a Bible Study meeting – and disperses again, its members doing other things with other people at other times, or perhaps doing little or nothing for long stretches.

The tasks come in different types, and may be few or many according to the style and tradition of the congregation and its leaders. Some are probably universal. There are tasks of governance: Kirk Session meetings, other committees, office-bearers going about their business. There are tasks relating to worship: the preparation and conduct of services, music, the sacraments. There are pastoral tasks: the conduct of the ordinances of religion (especially weddings and funerals) and usually the visiting of members and of parishioners in particular need. Beyond these standard activities the range and likelihood of other things varies so much that the outsider cannot presume anything about any congregation without paying attention to its particular life. Routines one congregation could not imagine existing without may be quite unknown somewhere else: children's work, weekday activities, congregational organisations, social services to the surrounding community, religious outreach. These and dozens of other ways of being busy form patterns of congregational life which never exactly repeat between any two churches in Scotland.

In each community, though, however minimal or sophisticated its corporate life may be, the things that happen have to be made to happen. The community has to shape itself to ensure that its stuff happens, to achieve whatever it achieves.

Theories of how organisations do things are interesting tools to apply to a reading of the life of the Church. A simple theory that fits this task particularly well is the Royal Navy's teaching on 'Command, Leadership and Management'. Everyone in the Service encounters this instruction, sometimes explicitly in classes addressing the concept as a subject in its own right, and often buried in other training or assessment at many points in the sailor's career. As a specialist topic CLM covers all the theories and thinkers you might expect to encounter, and presentations are predictably bedevilled by diagrams, acronyms and memorable analyses of human action and institutional forms. It is not necessary to plunge into such detail here: those three categories provide enough stimulus to make it easy to recognise congregations we have known.

In the Royal Navy

In the military world, command is an instrument held by an individual by virtue of the formal status, seniority or function they have been given by the organisation. It enables them to state what a subordinate in the same organisation must do, and is backed up with a power of compulsion over the person so commanded. Without the rank each holds in the Royal Navy and the censures available within the system, command means nothing. It is the authority to compel based on the stripes on one's sleeve. It works perfectly well when those commanded are willing, the situation is unthreatening, or the order is trivial and inconsequential. By itself it is dangerously inadequate in situations where men and women must have their reluctance overcome, their courage bolstered, their actions especially motivated.

The military machine, like any other organisation, needs to be managed. There need to be administrative systems that move things and people, train officers and ratings, resource operations and exercises, and do thousands of other tasks to ensure the Navy is doing a job and not just providing a museum-piece for the nation. Management is a perfectly respectable form of military activity, and most of the time most of what is happening in any ship or establishment is the management of something by someone tasked with ensuring some specified outcome. By the ordering of resources, the sequencing of events, the authorising of actions, the machine works. This is the authority to produce results based on the use of human intelligence and skill. It suffers the same limitations as command does, though, when the circumstances are frightening, unusual or unanticipated, and when people desperately need a good reason to take risks.

Leadership, though, is the mysterious quality of those whose authority does not rely solely on what is on their sleeve or in their brains. It is sometimes defined as the ability to get people to do willingly those things they would not otherwise wish to do. To some extent it can be developed as a leader is trained and proved, but many believe there needs to be an initial seed that no-one can plant and no-one can guarantee. Would I follow that lieutenant into a smoke-filled compartment if he were the leader of the fire-fighting team, without a word of command on his part? It is the authority to produce results based on character, charisma, trustworthiness and unarguable principles. It is the only hope in situations where those whose job is to follow have lost all other resources of security, courage, judgement or practical options. Any military unit can last a remarkably long time without it, but only if nothing very exciting is happening.

Within the life of the Royal Navy, management techniques are taught in different specialisms. Command is conferred through the system of promotions, conferred unilaterally by the system on the individual who is recognised as deserving their new authority. Leadership, however, is the constant theme of career development, support and training. The junior officer challenged to run a social event in the Wardroom, or the rating put in charge of a transport schedule, are being given the chance to prove – and improve – themselves and their standing. Those who draw them forward and give them their opportunities probably know at first meeting which raw trainees will one day be the leaders even they would follow into that smoke-filled compartment.

In the Church

Perhaps ministers, office-bearers and congregations you have known have already begun to flit through your mind.

In all those congregational organisms mentioned earlier, it is obvious that the first question to be asked is whether any of this is needed, whether anything is happening, whether there is anywhere to be led, whether there is anything to be managed.

There may quite respectably be no initiatives, nothing except a self-sustaining cycle of perfectly acceptable and welcome routine. In the small remote parish, the minister may have worked out a pattern of pastoral care that leaves everyone very content. Busy farmers may be grateful that there is no expectation of weekday meetings or groups to be joined or maintained or run. The Sunday service may be a smooth process in the hands of a few reliable people who know just what to do. It may, in short, be a gem of a parish ministering with perfect simplicity and effectiveness; and it would be a crime to mess about with it.

Ministers have many reasons for ill-judged busy-ness. Some believe that their ministry cannot be called a success unless there has been in it some identifiable initiative. Some find it easier to busy themselves with new tasks than to succeed at the standard old ones. A few worshippers who like novelty and fresh challenge will be so inspired by the resulting buzz that they will thrive and prosper in their church membership. Many people, who thought their church was the place to find familiar, gentle comfort, would prefer that things did not keep changing around them so much, so often.

Ministers equally have many reasons for ill-judged lack of new initiatives. Some know they are not charismatic enough to overcome the conservative personalities of those around them in the congregation's leadership. Some do not have the energy or the imagination to meet the obvious needs of the community. This time, the congregation will divide between those who are relieved not to be challenged and those who are frustrated by what they see as spiritual atrophy all around them.

The point is that one should never fixate on how to lead without first asking, in each situation, whether to lead, whether there is something to be done, to be fixed, to be begun. A young minister seeking his first charge told the Nominating Committee of a small community that he didn't do gimmicks and he didn't do projects and he didn't do schemes. He preached ordinary sermons set in familiar services, he visited those who needed to be visited, he was diligent in the work of the Presbytery and the General Assembly when it was his turn to go, and he would be a natural part of the local community. The Committee pounced, and the congregation was thoroughly happy. Things did slowly change, when they needed to, but never just for the sake of change.

Sometimes the depressing pressure to be seen to do something stems from a wearisome sense of duty about certain activities. There has to be a choir, there has to be a Sunday School, there has to be a Bible Study, there has to be a Guild. There has to be each of those things, however much wheedling, cajoling, threatening, rewarding or blackmail it takes to recruit the people to run it. No, actually, there does not need to be any such thing.

One of the liberating conclusions of the 'Church Without Walls' Special Commission in 2001 was that activity should follow vocation and not the other way round. If the person being thumb-screwed into hosting a Bible Study harbours a secret desire to undertake a sponsored cycle-ride for Tear Fund, how much more energetically and successfully they will fulfil their own dream than your grinding sense of duty. If the reluctant choir bass is a technical wizard who could run the sound-system so that – golly – the speakers can be heard clearly by the hearing-aid users, let the poor man out of prison, for pity's sake. Providence will somehow ensure the unglamorous jobs are done too, probably by the people willing to do their share alongside the things that make them feel most alive.

The minister is not always the culprit, the wielder of the shoe-horn, the petrifier of programmes. Sometimes the minister is the victim of other people's expectations. The culprits may be other office-bearers, who for reasons of ancient loyalty (or sheer lack of imagination) cannot see the congregation life in any other shape, or moving in any other direction, or travelling at any other speed. The victim may be the very person who ought above all to be the leader, but who is corralled by expectations and habits into deadening routines, or even bounced into change for change's sake by those whose bidding she has not realised she does.

We see it most easily though in ministers, whose roles we think we know, and who produce such expectations. We engage with it most deliberately with the only people who go through a process of interview and selection before they are given the leadership of a congregation. We worry about it most intensely when we think about those who tend to be blamed when congregational life is out of control, or moribund. Perhaps though, the characterisations that follow might work just as well for other kinds of leader, the ones who come free with the charge, the ones who can outstay almost any minister.

The Command Style

There is a style of ministry that Anglicans call 'Father knows best', in which the rector is invested with an authority by virtue of office, ordination, seniority, or a habit of congregational deference to the clergy. In the Presbyterian world none of those causes should be routinely found, but there are nonetheless ministers who bear themselves with the authority of command and relate to those around them with no expectation of discussion or the exchange of points of view. Anything that conceivably can be decided by the minister is decided by the minister alone, with the Kirk Session left to do only those things the law of the Church explicitly requires of it and nothing more.

There is much to commend this approach. The congregation probably runs with unmistakable efficiency and even effectiveness; for everyone knows what to do without stopping to argue about it, and serves a single vision that produces a great consistency of style and effect. The force of personality of one central figure can often neutralise the damaging potential of others who are not good team players and need firm handling. If the source of the command style is the self-awareness of greatly superior ability, the results may be highly visible excellence, often in preaching and the conduct of worship. The virtuoso is a delight to behold, and the price is worth paying.

Disaster can strike when a strong personality arrives – perhaps another member of a ministry team, or an experienced elder moving into the area – who cannot endure dictatorship no matter how successful, benign or creative it might be. Where the commanding figure does not support that with the innate ability to lead, it does not take much to remove the emperor's new clothes from the charismatic presence. The impact of that upon a congregation that might have built itself around a cult of the individual can be devastating.

Disaster strikes more often when the command-style minister reaches the end of her ministry, and leaves a ghastly hole in the middle of the congregation's existence. Into the power vacuum there is no knowing what forces will rush, and the next minister will inherit a community that might as well have been scourged by a flash-flood and needs to be re-built completely.

Disaster strikes – or rather, slowly overwhelms – when the figure in command lacks the qualities to use the command well. Where the style is not accompanied by any substance, direction is utilised purposelessly, and people are being told to do things for the sake of being told, and not to serve some clear end in view. And in the occasional circumstance when the central figure is wrongly motivated by personal gain or laziness or something worse, the willingly obedient may be horrified to discover where they end up.

And if the comparison with military life is useful, disaster strikes when the congregation is faced with some catastrophe that cannot be repaired by instructions and directions. When major physical or civic disaster befalls an unprepared town, religion takes on the paradoxical role of hero and villain. ('There cannot be a God if this has happened. We need to have a church service for the village.') Creative megalomania will not meet that need, will not substitute for long hours of pastoral care, will not find the right words, will not supply the presence that is noticed and appreciated.

In the Church as in the Navy, command has its place and neither institution could float, move and fight without it. But it is not everything; and it is not enough.

The Management Style

A large, complicated and busy congregation needs to have its activities managed. People, space, and financial and physical resources have to be co-ordinated to avoid asking the impossible of diaries, rooms and budgets. Someone has to do that, and it probably should not be the inducted minister. The tempting aphorism here is 'If you want something to be done right, do it yourself'; and the minister who has organisational talents may very well be able to arrange his congregational life far better as a result of his intelligent touch.

The Church of Scotland runs and re-runs an unwinnable argument between those who wish it was more business-like in its efficiency, and those who are appalled at the idea of the Church as a business (when patently the Body of Christ cannot possibly be anything so crassly commercial). Both sides have laudable, spiritual reasoning: one cannot bear to see the resources of the Church being used inefficiently and its service of the world needlessly hampered, while the other fears that the wrong measures will be used to understand our purpose and calling.

Many congregations contain people whose strengths are not in making things happen but in making them happen well. The shy member who could not be persuaded to join a committee, but who makes a perfect job every week of copying the recording of the service to circulate to the housebound; the paid secretary who has no interest in attending worship on a Sunday, but gets the minister to the right place at the right time every time; the Session Clerk who is not a great confidant of the minister but makes complete sense of the choreography for the quarterly communion; these are people who guarantee that the church's life is business-like where it needs to be without selling its soul. Only sometimes might someone like that be the minister.

The Leadership Style

The minister who is a born leader of others is an exciting, dangerous phenomenon. He owns a power he probably cannot really control, because his quality is so innate that he cannot help but be an inspiration and model. It is an authority that works by pull and not by push, because his actions draw people towards him, towards the things he champions, towards the activities and people he prioritises. He does not choose the moment at which he starts to be followed, and scarcely knows when he may be horrified to find people close behind him trusting where he is leading. He carries the heavy burden of being the figure of admiration.

Probably part of his reputation comes from the very fact that he does not command, because he does not need to and it is probably a foreign concept to him. Probably part of his reputation comes from the fact that he manages his time and energy with such discreet self-discipline that it is not the public hallmark of his ministry.

Such a minister is disproportionately likely to be an easily-hurt, thin-skinned soul, because he is sensitive to the feelings and opinions of others, and supremely self-critical. He does not bully because he does not need to, and he has profound respect for other the other people he works with and for. He has the happy knack of finding the right balance between personal authority and consultation: he knows when it is right and safe to stop at a point of decision and make the call, alone if necessary.

But even such a paragon of ideal leadership is not immune from disaster. The popular publications on self-improvement have in recent years discovered the concept of 'followership', and teach its importance alongside leadership in a functioning organisation. Good followers may include some of those who make the good managers in the congregation's weekly life, but may include people who are themselves leaders in other places but know that their place is different here. The captain of industry who prefers to remain in the lower deck with the Maritime Reserves chooses to be a follower in this world though he has all the responsibility of leadership in his civilian career. The prominent leader of society who is content not to be a leader in the Church may be far more refreshed by doing more receiving than giving, and more equipped for a difficult professional life by avoiding the piling-up of religious responsibilities.

Bad followers cannot recognise gifted leadership and get in the way of the achievements that ought to be possible. A bad follower may have such a fixed determination for the wrong priority that the minister ends up redirecting energy to deflecting that determination, and lose all the good momentum he once had. A bad follower may resent not being a leader, a status he has not an earthly chance of attaining because he just does not possess those ineffable qualities you cannot buy. He will oppose the real leader, and damage many people in doing so.

And yet, when it works, one can only admire the congregation with such an advantage. Few members of the Church would quite have the confidence to describe themselves as able to follow Jesus Christ without a guide between Him and them, an example to copy who is accessible and familiar and living a recognisable life in their real world. Where a stunning example of unfussy holiness and achievable goodness exists in the heart of the congregation's life, all things are possible.

And somehow the people survive when the ministry ends. They have been drawn into patterns they know how to repeat alone. They are not mindless slaves waiting for the next instruction and unable to function without one; so they can continue to evolve patterns and shapes when left alone.

A congregation rich in able people had mixed feelings when its minister was nominated to be Moderator of the General Assembly. They were a little nervous to lose their leader and teacher for such a period, knowing he would return after 15 months' sabbatical and they would be making an account to him in due course for the state of their church. A voice of wisdom spread the message around: 'We'll be all right, because he leads from the back. We will manage without him for this short time; that's how good a leader he is.'

What does the perfect ministry look like? That would depend on the congregation, and what it needed to do and what it wished to do. It would depend on the mixture of people 'making the stuff happen' there: who of them were themselves leaders, who were managers, who were the commanders who are sometimes needed even in religious life. It would depend on the bad or good luck of the congregation: cursed by key figures whose default mode is conflict with the direction of travel of the rest, or blessed by harmony of purpose and personality.

The blend of command, leadership and management must be unique in each congregation and to each ministry exercised there. There may come a moment when it is simply necessary to say 'because I say so'; but that is risky if it is used too often, or used by someone who has no other authority on which she may rely. There may come a time when it is only sensible to say 'oh here, let me organise that properly', to de-guddle an important issue and restore forward movement; but that is irresponsible when it is the default activity of someone who should be doing much more difficult and worthwhile things. But the greatest of them all, dangerous and terribly undesirable to men and women of sense and thought, is the experience of being trustingly followed, sometimes by people who deeply disagree on a big issue but are not deflected even by that in face of sheer inspiration and godly example.

Pen portrait

The Clerkship of this Presbytery would be a sight easier if there weren't quite so many requests for information from 121. The desk is simply no longer big enough for the piles of paper, piles of things needing to be done by other people's arbitrary deadlines. Every year is the same, all those e-mails from different departments wanting things to be counted, congregations to produce statistics, numbers to be attested, facts to be recorded. And every year come the same grumpy reminders from the Church Offices, pointing out that things are still awaited, expecting you to have everything you need from all the Session Clerks all at once, comparing you to other Presbyteries.

And there is this expectation that Clerks will learn bits of software they use for only one purpose in the year, and that is just to suit someone in Edinburgh. In a Presbytery as small as this one, it really would be a better use of time to type things straight into an e-mail. If there is some fancy database in George Street, someone there surely can type out the information again. There are better things to be done, in a parish like this, than other people's IT.

If the goalposts didn't keep moving it could just about be done. If they left us in peace to do things the same way from one year's end to another, we'd know where we were. One year someone has changed the way the accounts are supposed to be kept. The next year they decide our number of ministers has to changed and we have to start all over again to calculate the Presbytery Plan. Then the Assembly decides to fiddle with tenure, or the retirement age, or who can preach; and we hardly know what we can do around here.

There are some Clerks who do the job as if they had no other responsibilities to juggle, and who're fazed by nothing. They are the really annoying types whose minutes are polished 24 hours after the meeting, whose statistics are magically to hand as soon as they are requested, who seem to have a system for everything, a check-list for everything, a time-table for everything. No doubt they have empty desks, most of them; they'll be that type.

Mind you, there are compensations. You're the one person in the Presbytery who sees everything that goes on in the committees, and you can join it all up and really know what's going on in the area. You get to see all the ministers at work, and you soon know which ones have safe hands and which ones do more harm than good.

But then of course it's the ones doing the harm who cause you a lot of extra work, and it's no fun when things have gone really badly wrong somewhere and everybody assumed the Presbytery Clerk will just tell them what to do to make it all come right, just like that, as if it was easy.

And then you're back where you started, fixing other people's problems, making other people's lives work.

Filling a Vacancy

After I had formed the concept of this piece and before I had the chance to begin to write it, there appeared by coincidence a short article in the closed-circulation professional discussion sheet 'Ministers' Forum'. The author challenged people in vacant charges to think how they would present their congregations to potential applicant ministers, and began to suggest there might be an interesting, inverted way of considering the relationship of vacancy and minister. This essay takes the same idea further.

Ministers of all generations have tales to tell of their brushes with Vacancy Committees (nowadays called Nominating Committees). The funnier the story is, the more it is probably an indictment of the standards of process some congregations see fit to use. A probationer many years ago found himself in a small room being interviewed by three representatives of a rural charge he had never visited. The local Presbytery was in the middle of adjustment in the area, running that process bizarrely in parallel with the recruitment of the new minister. Now the probationer knew little about anything, of course; but he had a vague sense that something was wrong when the interviewers were unable to name the charge or state whether it possessed a manse. Such was the confused state of the adjustment process, that here was a Vacancy Committee earnestly trying to persuade a foolish baby minister to buy a pig in a poke.

A more common error by far is the expectation by a vacant congregation of finding the perfect minister no congregation has yet had, or by the available minister of finding the Church of Scotland's only flawless congregation.

Finding a human minister

No amount of experience of past ministry seems to cure some congregations of the intention of recruiting a perfect minister, able to undertake a series of tasks so extensive that it would more than fill his or her waking hours. No amount of relevant experience in other walks of life seems to dissuade intelligent church leaders from expecting the next minister to lack the last one's flaw but have no other flaws of his own. No amount of leadership from the Interim Moderator or guidance from the Presbytery's Advisory Committee seems to break the determination of some to recruit to a job-description so detailed that it simply is not the Ministry of Word and Sacrament, a job-description that never includes 'just love them'. The risk is that the Nominating Committee is so attracted to the applicant who knows how to appear on first encounter to be exactly what they think they want, that they do not give close enough attention to the quirky, off-beat, unconventional minister, or even in some places just the female, foreign or disabled minister, the minister who will leave people wondering 'how did we do that, how did we get there, where did that miracle come from?'.

Nominating Committees have great fun and great success when they set their sights on finding a minister who is a fallen, fragile human being, someone so much like themselves that they can imagine being loved by him or her. Nominating Committees are excited by their work when they exclude no-one, and allow themselves conversations they would never have dreamed of with people they had never imagined. Nominating Committees take pleasure in saying to their Kirk Sessions 'you're not going to believe who the new minister is going to be'.

Requiring an acceptable minister

Committees can no longer declare their preferences in areas that are protected by anti-discrimination rules. Much as they would love to reduce their work by ruling out in advance those who do not match the desired age, sex and marital status, they are compelled to waste everybody's time by going through the motions of seeing everyone who applies, and finding a persuasive – or if not persuasive then at least technically legitimate – reason not to appoint them. They can, however, limit the scope of applications by specifying in advance the theological style they believe is the only acceptable one. With the help of an Interim Moderator who has played the game before, they produce an advertisement in code, which every other minister can read and use to select genuinely possible opportunities.

You might think that every minister has a Bible-teaching ministry, to some extent or another, in some style or another. Yet the use of the word 'Bible' in a vacancy advertisement usually sends the message that the congregation requires a minister from one end of the Church's theological spectrum. Or rather, it indicates that the Committee has decided that the congregation ought to require such a minister; which might come as a surprise to the congregation or not, depending on quite a few things. Conversely, the word 'inclusive' in the advert, describing the breadth of the congregation or its work in the community, is code for a liberal position in the current debate on human sexuality and implies a welcome to those who are the subject of that controversy.

Whatever helpful nods and winks are given, they are based on the presumption that the searching congregation should set the terms, limit the search, determine who is or not to be given a realistic hearing. There is here a restriction on the potential for unexpected matches, and it is a restriction coming from one side of the communication, the side that gets to make the first move. It takes a bold minister to refuse to be put off by the signals, and to insist on applying anyway, perhaps genuinely or perhaps out of a gritty determination not to allow that part of the system to work. Two female ministers serving together on a committee designing the Church's anti-discrimination rules realised that a very prestigious city congregation (very prestigious according to itself, you understand, which is how these things always go) was in the process of advertising for a minister and was extremely unlikely to choose a woman. It was all they could do to resist applying, and invoking their committee's new anti-discrimination instruments when neither (presumably) appeared on the short leet. But that, admittedly, would have not have been a genuine application, however satisfyingly it might have turned out.

Congregations, wittingly or not, slice up the Church's ministry and advertise themselves to only part of it; and then wonder why so few people apply.

Certainly, congregations are entitled to have certain core expectations of a minister. The University and Church will have educated and trained him, and allowed him to get to the point of ordination only on being satisfied that he can reasonably preach, administer and offer pastoral care, study and work reflectively, and interact with those with whom he is meant to engage. The universal minimum of the minister's job can reasonably be expected to be fulfilled by him. What else is it fair to require?

The congregation, because no two are the same, will have its own particular life, elements of its own local mission and ministry, which surround that irreducible minimum. The question is: why does the field of possible ministers have to be limited by the peculiarities of the congregation's current activities? If those distinctive local priorities exist because the congregation has a passion for them, does not the congregation themselves undertake them? If they exist because a previous minister insisted on them, has she not gone? What strange and wonderful new initiatives might be unleashed on the unsuspecting community when the Committee has the courage or inspiration to do something that seems rather crazy? What much-loved traditions might be blessedly put to sleep to everyone's private relief? If the evening service were put out of its misery - attended as it is by a dozen people who all attended faithfully in the morning but feel they are supporting the minister by maintaining the burden of her writing another sermon every week – what else might be done with the time that is saved? What, in short, could be lost or might be gained if the job specification is freed from the terrible grip of current expectations?

So congregations reduce the variety of applicants before their advertisement has so much as seen the light of day; and present a detailed mould into which the successful candidate will have to squeeze.

What does any such congregation look like to the outsider? What does it look like in the carefully-crafted and beautifully-printed parish profile? What does it look like to the local minister who will be phoned by potential applicants who have more sense than to rely on the profile alone? What does it look like to the Presbytery Clerk, who will be phoned by friends who are supervisors of probationers thinking of applying?

The Congregation

Just as ministers can be expected to possess a common core of training and competency, so a congregation is expected to have certain irreducible resources. These will include physical things: church building, enough people to provide the standard functions of congregational life, and tools of the trade like organs, hymn books, communion ware and so on. The minister will naturally pay particular attention to the manse, and if she is lucky will discover that the fabric committee has adopted the attitude that the manse should be in exactly the state of readiness they would expect of their own homes.

There are congregations whose physical infrastructure is inadequate to the task, and yet they still puzzle over their failure to recruit a minister. A vacant congregation has failed to renovate its elderly church building during its last three ministries, while almost every other parish in that half of the Presbytery has refurbished, rebuilt or replaced theirs. No doubt they will have a sense of unfairness if they do not quickly recruit a minister; but who will tell them why?

Ministers will look too to the invisible infrastructure, the team of people, and want to know whether and how it works. The Session Clerk whose well-meaning interference has frightened away the last two young ministers, the united congregation who are so little united that the two groups might as well wear contrasting rugby tops, the former minister living half a mile away and cheerfully agreeing to funerals and weddings; these things shout loudly. Some withdrawals of applications speak very well of the wisdom of that minister, and say everything about the congregation that does not know itself well enough, nor understands the game.

Only then, perhaps, if the congregation has survived scrutiny so far, does the applicant consider the job he or she will have to do. How many funerals per year? How many weddings per year? How many unavoidable, legitimate, parish weddings per year? How many schools, and how many of those inviting chaplaincy? How many care homes? How many Church of Scotland social care projects? What other churches, and what ecumenical expectation, burden or opportunity? What else is there that gives possibilities of all sorts: charities, community groups, political upheaval, twinnings (of church or community)?

What is a vacant congregation to do, faced with just few enough available ministers and probationers that no-one can easily assume their post will be filled? What is a vacant congregation to do, realising that in the real world – and not just in the fantasy of this essay – there are not piles of candidates to accept or reject, to short-leet and rank, to disappoint or delight?

There is a question a congregation can ask; the whole congregation, with Kirk Session and Nominating Committee and Interim Moderator and Advisory Committee and anyone else around who is willing to help them face the truth. Does this congregation deserve to have a minister? The answer will be 'no', if:

- The minister will be expected to live and work in conditions the Committee members would not accept in their own homes and work

- The minister will be expected to take back tasks currently done in the vacancy by congregational members who are perfectly capable of continuing to do them

- The minister, for that matter, will be expected to do any tasks that could be done by others, including newsletter editing, driving, furniture removal, catering and photocopying.

- The minister's spouse will be expected to do anything not expected of any other member of the congregation (that is, if he or she happens to be a member of the Church and chooses to be a member of that congregation)

- There is low-grade civil war amongst office-bearers, or unaddressed bullying on the broadest definition of it

- Any crying need has been unaddressed in the last three years, including the state of the buildings, the state of children's work, the distribution of jobs amongst office-bearers, the state of stewardship

- Anyone is foolish enough to declare, whisper or write 'The new minister must bring in young people'

A vacant congregation with no shortage of money, talent and leadership had persuaded itself that it would be irresistible to the very best of ministers, and that the most articulate, experienced and well-known preachers of the Church would queue up to be considered. To be minister of the congregation would require the diplomatic skills of the Secretary-General of the United Nations, because there was just too much articulate talent, too articulate by half. A well-known minister found himself preaching there during the vacancy, and spending some time after the service in conversation with elders and other members. Over coffee he found himself being backed into a corner of the Church building by the redoubtable Sir XY, who for years had pursued his pet projects so enthusiastically that they drained the blood from every other organisation and initiative in the place. By force of his personality and a capacity for the kind of lip-quivering disappointment described elsewhere in this book as disguised bullying, Sir X had everyone at his beck and call, and no-one could deny that he did very great good for very many people – even if the rest of the congregation was in a state of atrophy as a result. The visiting preacher left with two messages ringing in his ears. The first was from Sir X, that in the next ministry there would be no doubt that his projects must have the top priority because, goodness, they were so very deserving. The second was from some of the congregational leaders, that the preacher would be very welcome to apply for this charge that probably needed a strong hand and the ability to encourage and enable everyone's gifts. The preacher left in a cloud of dust and a fast car, not caring tuppence what the manse looked like or where his children would have gone to school.

A Future System?

History explains to us why vacant congregations have to recruit ministers as if they were businesses recruiting employees. For the first few centuries after the Scottish Reformation the minister was chosen by the patron of the parish, who might be the Crown, a local landowner or a burgh council. The local holder of power and authority chose the minister, because that was who paid them. In the modern era, that system has rightly disappeared, but the congregation – once able only to veto the patron's choice – has stepped in to that vacuum to become the choosing body, through its elected Nominating Committee.

Perhaps that is an accident of history that should be questioned. Other denominations do it differently: churches with individual bishops, or the Salvation Army with its strong tradition of rank, operate much more of a 'push' system, sending the minister to the place of their service. The Church of Scotland has almost entirely a 'pull' system, Biblically-based no doubt, where the local church calls its minister to them. It weakness is that congregations seem to be just as imperfect, broken and inadequate as the individuals who enter the ministry, but it is the flawed congregations in whom is placed all the power to choose. It is like dating, but as if only one partner may have a choice. Must this be?

So what would happen if, on the day that pigs fly, the system could be inverted? Try this.

Ministers and probationers could make themselves available through a central system of intimation of availability, accessible only to the elected congregational Committees. There would be no need for individuals' names to be used, and no intimation of age, sex, marital status or any other issue protected by anti-discrimination law. They would be free to indicate their style of ministry, theological preference, or any other information that might help them to find an ideal match. Ministers could make themselves available to engage in due course with vacancies whilst remaining anonymous in these earlier stages. The congregations' Committees would now be the applicants, allowed each to have only three applications live at any time. A period would be permitted for the usual process of meetings, hearing the individual conduct worship, and so on, but with the individual taking the lead.

And then the applicants would choose their preferred congregations. The decision would be made in consultation with the people who would be most affected – the people with so little influence at present – spouse and children. After all, no-one in a congregation will have to change their paid employment when the new minister comes; but the minister's spouse might. No child in the congregation will have to change their school when the new minister comes; but the minister's children might. No elderly member of the congregation will find their support package changed when the new minister comes; but the minister's elderly mother might. And the minister would choose the congregations that deserved to have a minister, deserved to have this minister.

The new system could overcome another of the most frustrating aspects of the existing one. Nominating Committees currently each work to their own timetable, different by a few days from others progressing at about the same pace, but handling applications from the same people. Too often, an applicant's second or third choice congregation makes an offer of nomination with a tight time-limit imposed for acceptance, too tight to make it possible to wait and discover whether one's first-choice of application has succeeded. On this imaginary new system, the intimation of available probationers and ministers would be made at a single point, and the interested vacancies given a time-frame on which to work. On a pre-arranged date when all the usual process had taken place, the individual would state to the central co-ordinator of the system his or her full list of preferences in order. Where two or more individuals had the same church as their first preference, that congregation's Committee would immediately choose between them, and the rest of the allocation would continue with the removal of those elements. There is still therefore a recognition that some charges are more popular and will therefore have some choice. Within a day or two the matching would be complete, and the arrangements handed over to the Presbytery for the normal process of call and sustaining of the appointment. Individuals who had not selected any congregation, or who chose only those congregations who had the luxury of taking the offer of another minister in the scheme, would start again on the next cycle six weeks later; and so would congregations who had not succeeded in selling themselves at all, and who if wise would put in some effort to produce a different result next time.

The system would not work; of course it wouldn't. A dozen technical and logistical problems would quickly bring it to its knees. The flight of fancy that produces it, however, has its point of departure in the current system that tells congregations they merit a power of hiring and firing. That is the only point of all this foolishness.

Even without a new system, could the 'Ministers Available' column of *Life and Work* ever contain adverts such as these?

Probationer minister, 20 years' prior experience in Social Work, preference for West Central Scotland, recent experience in UPA parish, reputation for developing people's campaigning abilities, seeks busy charge to absorb energy.

(No-one reading this knows that this probationer uses a wheelchair.)

Parish minister, ten years in current rural charge, family reasons for wishing to move to Aberdeen area, heavily committed in national committee work, seeks part-time parish with strong commitment to community involvement.

(No-one reading this knows that this minister came originally from another denomination in a Commonwealth country.)

Army chaplain, ordained six years, belongs to Forward Together, seeks charge with emphasis on expository preaching and commitment to overseas mission.

(No-one suspects that this minister is in fact a woman.)

And in reply might congregations send applications with covering letters like these?

> *Dear Colleague,*
> *We refer to your advertisement in the May edition of Life and Work and wish to be considered as the location of your next ministry.*
> *St Matthew's Parish recently achieved full status after five years as a New Charge Development on the East side of Glasgow. Located in an area of general poverty, with a very high number of asylum seekers in the population,*

the Church has come to be regarded as a place of refuge for people of many faiths and none, and its energetic and mainly young congregation has had to learn a great deal of legal expertise to support the most vulnerable in the community.

The Nominating Committee feels very strongly that this should be the place where you exercise your ministry, and that the work of the congregation will find a sure foundation if you will lead us. The congregation is willing to undertake to organise a rota to ensure that there is someone present in the Church centre through each day to support you when you are there or to represent the congregation when you are elsewhere, or to develop its ministry of presence in any way you suggest.

You are most welcome to attend worship in St Matthew's at any time, and advise us when it would be convenient for us to meet with you and answer your questions about our work and witness.

Yours sincerely,

Dear Colleague,

We refer to your advertisement in the May edition of *Life and Work* and wish to be considered as the location of your next ministry.

St Mark's was recently disjoined from its linkage with St Luke's, Laurencekirk, and as a part-time charge has recovered its original single-centre ministry to the farming country to the south of the town. The parish area coincides with the catchment area of a Primary School, which lies within easy walking distance of the new-built manse in the hamlet of Markstown.

The parish church, originally built in 1545 and with Grade A listed status, attracts many weddings each year. These generate fees producing a large surplus over the Mission and Aid allocation that is therefore easily met each year, and the weddings are conducted by a recently retired minister living in the area and employed for this specialist ministry.

Our Committee will be delighted to make arrangements for you to spend a weekend at a hotel a few miles away and to show you round the parish, church and manse. Your privacy is important to us, and we are proud of our record of confidentiality in our process to date.

Yours sincerely,

Dear Colleague,

We refer to your advertisement in the May edition of *Life and Work* and wish to be considered as the location of your next ministry.

Following the departure after thirty years' distinguished ministry of our previous minister, Dr D, on his appointment as Director of the EA's new Titus Project, we are anxious to help our next minister to discern their calling as soon as possible. In our times of prayer together the Nominating Committee has been convinced that we should be completely open to the guidance of the Holy Spirit and to the possibility that something new and beyond our attempts to control it might take place here at Smith Memorial Church.

With your experience in the army, working largely with unchurched young adults, we would be excited to meet you and discuss the concerns we have about teenagers in our parish, and the shape of our future mission to them in particular. This will of course be our task, but we know we need expert guidance, and believe you may be able to support us.

Our older members are particularly inspired by their energetic support of Tear Fund's work in central Africa, and would like to find ways to strengthen those links and foster personal contacts with missionaries in that part of the world.

When you have had a chance to pray about this letter, we look forward to hearing whether ours is one of the charges you would like to consider further.

Yours sincerely,

Pen portrait

Well that evening certainly wasn't like anything you'd normally get at church. Once we'd checked in and got our rooms sorted out, we looked at the Youth Assembly programme and found we were having a welcome meal in the dining room. You could hardly see from one end of it to the other, it was so huge. And it was full, yes I really mean full, of people around my age, and all of them from Church of Scotland congregations all over the country. Honestly, where I come from, I've not met 300 young Christians in my whole life adding them all up, and I've certainly never been in a room with that many all at once.

Actually, in the glen I come from, I've not been in a room with more than three Church members my own age, ever. It's hard work at school when there's almost no-one else who thinks the same way, and they say 'oh here we go again' when you talk about stuff that matters like Palestine, or mention things you do like running the bookstall after the morning service. And if we're being really honest, it's pretty hard work at church sometimes, when you think about the music and the words and the people who do everything. It always feels as if the under-20s are just being allowed to go to something that's actually for the old people, and never the other way round.

That's why this evening kind of blew our minds. There was just about nothing anyone else in my church would have liked, and I loved it all. They played – live! – the Christian songs I'd only heard on CDs, and they used them for worship, as if we were in church. They spoke about the places we came from and I discovered a hundred other people there who were each the only person from their church, and half of them were there for the first time like me. An older guy in jeans talked about the Bible but he used the words I'd use every day. And we sang this African song, sitting on the floor at the end of the night, with no band this time and very quiet, over and over again, and some people sang harmony with it, and some people stopped singing and just listened, and somehow for a few minutes I felt as if there was nothing in the way between me and God and I could think anything and let God hear it. I'd never felt anything like that before.

And if that lot would give a shock to the congregation back home, wait till they hear about tomorrow and the next day. We're going to debate things that we care about, and tell the whole Church of Scotland what we decided. We're going to be talking about Church membership and how we can help to attract people to our congregations. This weekend will give us a few ideas, I should think. We're having a debate about Palestine, and people are beginning to talk about it, and they all feel as strongly as I do. And you know, that seems to matter, really seems to matter, in this place.

Organised religion

In the congregations, clergy houses, theological colleges and fraternal groups of the Church of England or the Roman Catholic communion, the local bishop and the Church's hierarchy are never very far from conversation, part of the awareness of the worshipping community even when not present in person. A person – experienced, chosen, accepted, known – provides one convenient focus for the life of the Church in one area, provides a single point at which the authority of the Church is visible. When things go well he is the focus of unity and a source of inspiration, an encouraging figure representing the broader Church to those labouring in one small space within it. When things go badly he is the target of frustration and complaint, and at his door are no doubt laid some criticism that he deserves and much that he does not. The structure of the denomination is manifest in a person who relates to everyone who is striving to be the Church there and then, so their connection to the system is through a human relationship.

In the congregations, manses, divinity schools and local fellowships of the Church of Scotland, no individual exists to fulfil that role, to draw attention to a single point of focus in the structure of our Church. In times of success, there is no one central figure to lead the celebrations. In times of frustration, people choose many different targets for their anger or blame. All the Presbyterian has is an organisation that can be pictured in several shapes and populated in different ways. Some visualise themselves in a series of concentric circles that has the parish church in the middle, with the Presbytery and General Assembly surrounding them with support, supervision, resources, interference, interest, demands, and other things thickly supplying context and meaning to the central, local activity. The Church Without Walls Report championed this image. Some imagine themselves in a different series of concentric circles that has the national Church in the middle, with Presbyteries standing closer to the core and parishes around the outside, receiving the support, supervision and all the rest as things sent out to them to stop them falling off the edge. Members of the Church who talk about 'the Church' in the third person, not realising they are themselves part of the institution, probably work with this model. Some think of the Church in layers, highly conscious of its court structure and aware that the Presbytery has power of direction over the Kirk Session and congregation, while the General Assembly has the ultimate determination of questions affecting everyone. And some intuitive souls see no structure beyond the people and visible activities of the Church, and do not recognise the need for any human system of rules, norms and authorities in the Body of Christ present in the world.

Presbyterians are fondly accused by other Christians of respecting organisation in religion more than others do, and of having a more developed polity than exists in other Churches. In ecumenical settings, the Reformed Church representatives are somehow expected to have a special concern for meetings, minutes, rules and protocols. It might be a flattering reputation to have, but it is not merited. Other Churches have as many systems as Reformed Churches do: there are methods for appointing clergy, disciplining church leaders, allocating resources, measuring success, training for tasks, no more in one tradition than another, only differently achieved from place to place. With no individual figurehead standing between the observer and the legal structures, no bishop representing all the authority that is stacked behind him, Presbyterians can simply see the machinery running the life of their Church, and see its glory and its faults.

The Spirit and the Law

In every structured Church in every age, and in the national Church in today's Scotland, there always exists a school of thought that opposes the structures, rules, authorities – the very organisation itself – to the movement of the Holy Spirit to achieve new and amazing things and to form and reform the Church without limit of human imagination. The first Desert Fathers left every structure behind, and found a hermit existence free from every social constraint on their piety and obedience. Irish missionary saints set off with no support, utterly free to turn Europe on its head. Religious communities, from wandering friars to warrior Jesuits and enclosed mystics, were founded almost always by someone leaving the familiar and beginning again without their old rules. Still today on the edges of many communities of faith inside the Church of Scotland, people are bursting to express their faith in new ways without having to satisfy someone else's standards or defer to anyone who is not there, who does not see the Spirit move in this place, who is not part of the new movement, the new way of being the Church.

It seems important, though, to notice the logical flaw that imagines these are things that are opposed to each other. 'Organised religion' is not the opposite of 'spiritual initiative'. The opposite of 'organised religion' is only 'disorganised religion'. The opposite of 'spiritual initiative' might be 'spiritless initiative', and it might be 'spiritual inertia'. That is all. Whether a religious tradition is generally well organised or generally shambolic does not of itself determine whether the Spirit of God is present and whether change is possible. Good organised religion might provide the flexibility to seize signs of revival and hasten wonderful new things. Bad organised religion may stifle the most patently godly new idea and defend old ways relentlessly, and do awful damage and commit terrible sin. It is the manner of the organisation, not the fact of it, that makes the difference.

The Church over the long reach of ages keeps the tradition of patriarchs and apostles, trying to arrange their world in obedience to the expectations God placed upon them. Surely the Old Testament follows the efforts of a people identified by a code of living, grittily maintaining difficult laid-down patterns of interaction with each other, with strangers and with God. Under all the provocation any life can suffer – rootlessness, famine, conflict, slavery, civil unrest – a race of men and women recognised its very point and meaning in a structure of regulation. The code was not an obstacle to their walk with God but marked its path. The Law was not a distraction from spiritual growth but its means. In the generations of Jewish history where the people managed to resist choosing a personality, a king, a human star, they saw their place in the world by looking at the way their life was shaped uniquely for them as for no other people.

And surely the New Testament tells the shorter, explosive story of a new way of living with God, which burst out of the old so vigorously that some custodians of the old way feared and resisted it and believed it was a canker that could not remain there. From the very hour that Christ sent out the Twelve in pairs with a rule of simplicity and a plan of campaign, until the Apostles thrashed out agreement about a relationship with the old law and used international letter-writing to direct church life all over the Empire, the embryonic Church developed means, standards, consistent practices to ensure its faithfulness and its effectiveness.

Today our Church never ceases from wrestling with those demands, asking itself endless questions about the requirements it places on its people, straining to know the commandments to follow and see the means to keep that faith. How can the guardians of religious rules provide the ones that are needed, recognise the ones that impede progress, and all the while avoid idolising laws that turn out to be the creation of human skill and the object of human conceit?

Leaders and Rulers

All this struggle it places into the hands of those who are chosen to make its decisions: ministers of Word and Sacrament, professional deacons, and the elders of the Church in every parish. Rightly our Church finds men and women of great talent and many kinds of holiness, and excitedly marks them as preachers, teachers, evangelists, pastors and workers in many difficult and specialist tasks. Unavoidably our Church pours all these people into the categories of minister, deacon and especially elder; it seems to be the obvious way to acknowledge and honour them, to place them in the community as givers of some particular service. The problem is that many of these charismata belong in the Church but not in the governing of the Church, enliven the worshipping community but not – thank God - through its administration. Imprisoning those gifted spirits in the Church's courts is unkind to them, and anyway it is wrong for the Church. Those whose gift is discerning the gifts of others, and whose authority equips them to ordain others, need the moral courage to confer ordination only on those whose charism is one of leadership and governance. Ordination is not a prize for service given or a permission for future contribution, but it is the sign of bearing one particular burden and one only, the steering of the Church and the structuring of her means.

Ordination is for leaders. Appoint, then, those who may visit the old and frail; appoint those who help to ensure the Church is a welcoming and hospitable place; appoint those who handle property and money and complicated things most people would rather were not their duty. Do not ordain these though, except those who are policy-makers, judges, discerners and defenders of the way that all should follow. The number of leaders and governors God provides to any congregation really does not have to coincide with the number of districts into which the membership is divided for pastoral purposes; so do not keep ordaining up to that number come what may. The number of leaders and governors God provides to a particular congregation might not be predictable in relation to its size, so do not feel you must ordain many elders only because the congregation is large. The right number is exactly the number of men and women who have the gift of such wisdom, experience and vision that they can be trusted to judge what demands should be made of other faithful people in living out the calling of the whole Church. Ordain only these.

Theirs then becomes a role that brings scrutiny and suspicion, that bears other people's hopes and conflicting expectations, that often takes them to a point where it is not easy to choose the future rightly. Once again many metaphors abound: they are running a machine; or they are constructing the road ahead; or they are opening and closing doors; or switching on and off the sound of a voice. They are, no doubt, themselves listening for voices and indications and calling and instinct, so that they will do the right thing, the godly thing, in any time of difficult decision. In the Presbyterian setting that has no focal individual, what they represent is the object of the disappointments of those who feel frustrated in what they are trying to do. When the rules for distributing resources fails the person fired by a new idea, and when the rules for retirement ages separate a minister and congregation who wished to continue together a little further, and when the rules about preaching do not allow a completely new voice to speak out a prophecy that is heart-felt, over and over again that suspicion is felt, that the law of the Church, the government of the Church, the leaders of the Church cannot possibly be on the side of the saints.

Process and Abuse

And just occasionally that suspicion turns out to be right. In many Presbyteries, and in the General Assembly every year, some protagonists in the drama of debate abuse their good knowledge of process and procedure to achieve a technical victory over someone who is less experienced and sophisticated. A first-time commissioner at the Assembly is unaware of the Standing Order that says a motion involving new expenditure can be made only if a scheme for finding the cost out of the rest of the Church's central budget is also proposed. She has a dream, a religious passion, for a new project she can see would transform lives and encourage faith; and out of courtesy she approaches someone from the relevant committee to explain what she intends to move. The wily committee member says nothing about the Standing Order, knowing that the motion will fall foul of it and be ruled out of order by the Moderator. Luckily for the commissioner, her courtesy extends to providing the Clerks' table with a written copy of the motion; and when the Clerk notices the problem he helps her to re-word the proposal in more general terms to survive the challenge from the committee. Serve them right.

In some courts, the body tries to operate with no skeleton at all, no predictability, no way of guaranteeing that everything necessary has been done, no tidiness in its conduct. A minister and Session Clerk have many beautiful ideas for the service to welcome new elders to their sphere of service, and dismiss the all-too-familiar (they say) language of the Book of Common Order. Using inspiring and provocative language from another tradition, the minister commissions three members of the congregation to a new calling, but without the reading of legal texts or the putting of any vows he fails to ordain them. The three, and the whole congregation, are left feeling rather sad because the much-loved service of ordination – that would have so resonated in the memories of the other elders present – has been abandoned and no-one is quite sure whether the ordination has properly taken place. The passage of time, the elapse of the legal period to challenge its inadequacy, and as usual the grace of individuals to cover up the mess, takes care of it. Yet it never quite feels right.

In some courts rules and procedures are so excessively honoured by the organisation itself that the life of that body ossifies, becoming lifeless in the hands of fanatics. When a tiny Presbytery of twenty members is run as if it is a cumbersome Assembly of 850, with the tiniest and least contentious decision put to a counted vote, the most sensible and welcome adjustment of wording minuted as a separate amendment, and the most helpful contribution ruled out of order because of some Standing Order about numbers of speeches, the Holy Spirit seems to be presented with a slalom to negotiate – which is not an ideal course for a wind blowing where it wills.

Process and Progress

If ever, though, there were a body that learned over time to grasp the spirit of good process but fend off all attempts to stultify it with minutiae, it is the National Youth Assembly of the Church. Hundreds of older teenagers and younger adults have met each year to reflect on the most difficult challenges lying ahead of the Church, to elect representatives to the General Assembly, and to develop their skills as part of the up-coming leadership of the whole Church locally and nationally. The development of its ways has been inspiring. The first two or three Youth Assemblies in the mid-1990s used actual General Assembly reports complete with actual Proposed Deliverances, were moderated by General Assembly Moderators, and probably flew straight over the tops of the heads of younger and less process-fixated members. They were heaven for a few, and the rest no doubt enjoyed everything outside the debates. The next few Youth Assemblies, at the beginning of the new decade, still borrowed topics and suggestions from the General Assemblies' materials, but produced their own proposals, appointed Moderators from their own ranks, and found ways to involve far more of the members. It was still like walking a very strong dog, trying to stop those who loved the tiny details of debate from pulling everyone into the technicalities they loved to play with for their own sake. Eventually the Youth Assembly found its way of working, entirely separate from the Principal Clerk's office. They tackle important themes they identify themselves, moderated by one of their own and clerked by another. They debate substance and know how to avoid wasting time on details so tiny they can better be left to the General Assembly to fix. They produce a list of ideas the leadership of the wider Church wishes they had not thought of, because they are so wise and difficult and sometimes irresistible.

From time to time the formal courts of the Church catch that instinct, and let the processes before them serve their mission. A minister, let us imagine, intends to retire at 65 without wishing to invoke the rules that might allow an extension of her ministry for a few more years. As the time approaches she discovers that her adult son must undergo treatment for cancer and be cared for by her for six months. A change of circumstances and a house-move would be disastrous, and she is distraught. Surrounded by a loving congregation and a compassionate Presbytery, she discovers that an application is being prepared by the Presbytery Clerk for an extension to her ministry in terms of the regulations, along with another one for a compassionate leave of absence for the first ten weeks of her son's treatment. Everyone knows those rules were not designed for this; everyone, including every member of the Presbytery who unanimously approve both applications and offer to share the congregation's pastoral care for those months.

Or a congregation, let us imagine, is gradually losing its way and its new minister lacks the qualities of leadership needed to grip its difficulties and heal its malaise. Neither the situation nor the minister is so bad that the Presbytery could easily initiate any emergency action, but the Superintendence Convener is beginning to hear of the unease in the parish, to see more and more children transferring into his own neighbouring Sunday School, and to notice the slump in financial giving over the last twelve months. The rota for routine superintendence visits is due to be prepared for the coming year, and the Convener quietly slips the congregation to the top of the list, though it is not strictly their turn to be visited. More, after all, can be formally uncovered when searching questions are asked than by waiting for the situation to produce anything so brave as a complaint.

Or a tiny congregation in a remote location and part of a linkage, let us imagine, has a Kirk Session that consists only of the minister and three elders. One elder is ill and the other two are infamous for their life-long suspicion of each other. The minister is at his wits' end, and cannot begin anything new and creative. The Presbytery has used its imagination to find ways to bring the situation to its official attention, and the Business Convener proposes that two elders from the minister's other Kirk Session be appointed assessor elders to their neighbour for one year, to lift it off its feet by sheer weight of numbers and make change possible at last.

Flexibility and common sense extend to the guardians of the texts of the laws in the Church's administration, who relish the challenge to remove obstacles or invent new instruments of grace for the Church's work. They too are ministers and elders and members of congregations trying to follow the one who said 'follow me' without their feet being tangled in fascinating processes that only slow them down. Their gift at its best is the ability to think linearly as lawyers, and laterally as saints, in the same breath.

In 2000 the Church's Procurator designed a new system for the discipline of the few ministers who make misjudgements too serious to be ignored by the Church. A process emerged that passed muster with spiritual standards, human rights charters, Presbytery authority, people's perception of their own ability to handle such difficult cases, and the best possible practice in hearing and adjudicating on evidence. In the ensuing years, as the first handful of cases washed through the new system like oil going through a new engine, the rough edges were gradually smoothed by many tiny amendments brought to the General Assembly by its Legal Questions Committee and approved on each occasion by the wider Church.

The process was an uncomfortable, heavy endurance-test for those denying the allegation made against them, who had to undergo every part of the process in the legislation. It struck the Committee that the experience was no better for ministers willing to admit all or part of the allegation and accept the censure of the Church without resistance. There was no abbreviated process in those cases, no motivation built into the process for people who might be persuaded to own up quickly to their ethical mistakes. What was needed was what the lawyers unofficially labelled the 'it's a fair cop' amendment, and no sooner was the omission spotted than it was filled. Now the procedure, still of course a horrible experience, is at least a much faster one for those who have already reached the point of admission and repentance, and deserve to be treated accordingly. In years to come the process will probably be polished and improved further, because the legislation is a living text flexing to meet the needs of the Church in its most difficult and sensitive situations.

Process and Vocation

Facing ordination, standing on the brink of ministry, diaconate or eldership, the Church member has a tumult of thoughts crashing around inside: thoughts about spiritual adequacy and personal worthiness, thoughts about responsibilities to others and opportunities for service, thoughts about the routine ahead and the burden to be picked up in the coming days, and thoughts about all those rules and procedures and what is going to be expected. Those who are not lawyers are tempted to avoid all engagement with those latter things, either persuading themselves it is a distraction from the Gospel to focus on the Law, or just blanking it all out of fear of confusion or failure. Those who take a deep breath and apply themselves to discover how the governance works and how to make it work for good – and they quickly discover they do not need to be lawyers to achieve that – are the people who hold the levers of change throughout the Church. They are the ones who can make a business meeting inspire those who attend it; they are the people who can deal with a dispute quickly; they are the Presbytery officials who know how to speed up a vacancy; they are the staff members who can find resources to make someone's dream come true. They are the spirits who sometimes, maybe just sometimes, clear all the gates away from the path of the Spirit blowing through the Church and abiding by no human rules. It is the humans who make up the Church who will achieve very little in chaos, and who need all the help they can give one another to discover the ways that work.

Pen portrait

I'd never stopped to think much about the business side of the Kirk. I've always known it needed quite a lot of money, and I've always given what I could. In the spring time they had the annual meeting every year, and you could see in the accounts where all the income came from and where all the expenditure went. In between I didn't think much about it.

And when somebody decided they had to put in disabled access, and somebody else decided it would be a grand time while they were at it to develop the whole vestibule to make it a bit more welcoming, I fairly enjoyed getting involved in that fund-raising and seeing what a difference it made. And maybe I did chip in a few ideas about the furniture and the colour of the paint, but no-one seemed to mind. I suppose I began to realise what a responsibility it is for the Board to look after a great big building like this, as well as the hall and the manse.

So it seemed pretty natural to agree to Kath's suggestion that she'd nominate me at last Sunday's meeting as a new member of the Board. I made it clear they mustn't be expecting any great expertise from me; but I could give them some time, and I suppose I know all the local businesses pretty well, and I've been around the congregation for a long time now and I know all of them too.

I hope people aren't looking at me and thinking 'who does she think she is?' though. I'm not one for spouting religious stuff, and the Kirk had better not expect me to do all that bit. I wouldn't be an elder, not on your life. But we need to take our turns at the down-to-earth jobs, and I've not done my bit like this before. You come along every Sunday and you're supposed to think about what you can do for God; and it's sometimes hard to know what you should think about or offer to do. The Church is there for you at the highs and lows, and I've needed help from them more than once, to be sure. It's not so easy sometimes to know what you can do in return. So this is grand, really, even if it's a wee bit scary to start with.

It's going to be fun, I think, to see how people behave in those meetings, whether it's just the same as they do the rest of the time. Take Julie: she's the Treasurer in the Kirk and the Treasurer in the WRI. I bet if getting money out of her for anything in the Rural is like blood out of a stone, she's probably just the same here. No wonder it took a few extra Board meetings to get the funds in place for the vestibule. Well, that's what I heard. Or what about Ian: if I've heard him go on once about those old hymn-books given in memory of his father who died in nineteen oatcake... I bet getting CH4 will be 'over his dead body' as long as he's on the Board. Och listen to me, worse than Miss Marple.

It's going to be fun, though.

Churches Together

Some people are deeply troubled by the multiplicity of Churches, and believe that Christ's longing for unity amongst his followers produces for us a fundamental Christian mandate. Some denominations officially take the same view. Other individuals would not sacrifice their confidence that their own tradition is right and others are wrong, and would not risk their purity for what they see as the less important principle of unity. Some denominations officially take that view.

The first tragedy of the modern ecumenical movement lies in the fact that its protagonists have so many different models of Church unity; and the variety of these approaches rivals the depth of difference of view on all the questions of faith and order that produced all those divisions in the first place. What to do about disunity can itself be a cause of disunity, within Churches as well as between them. Debates about method, occupying those most devoted to the movement, leave colleagues back home disillusioned and alienated and inclined to believe resources would be better applied to their Church's own mission and ministry. The number of detailed models may be limited only by the number of specialists who think about these things; but several types repeat over the years and across the worldwide Church.

The first and most ambitious model desires to reduce the number of identifiable ecclesial entities ('Churches' as denominational units), by uniting two or more wherever it can be done. A second and different way of achieving new entities is to create new organisations that involve more than one Church, but without losing the participating denominations: these may take the form of social care agencies, academic units, lay training institutes, retreat centres, ecumenical agencies. The third type of initiative does not produce any new legal entity, but consists of actions, initiatives and projects jointly undertaken: a shared service for a special festival, a representative sent to a national event to represent more than one local congregation, the staffing of one Church's project by members of another in a time of stretch. The final model is simply an attitude of friendship that fosters personal relationships of clergy or members, taking care not to put obstacles in each other's paths, taking care not to give a public impression of opposition to each other. Most ecumenical projects will largely fit at least one of these types.

Each of these patterns has been evident nationally, amongst the hierarchies and central structures of Western Churches, and locally wherever more than one tradition ministers to the same place or population. The second tragedy of the ecumenical movement has been obvious whenever vast energy is put into pursuing one hopeless model, energy that would have borne fruit if put into another. The choice is driven by the underlying philosophy being followed.

Church Union

In Scotland, the first and most difficult 'Church unity' model is out of favour, suffering the especially deep obscurity that inevitably follows for a while the failure of any extra big attempt to make it work. The Scottish Church Initiative for Union (SCIFU) reminded all its participants what a terrible journey that is to attempt, and what a great capacity for courage and disappointment is needed in its travellers.

The starting-point for any process like that is an intelligent but surely rather wistful grasping of each partner's current reality. Such a reality will embrace many aspects of Church life: doctrinal statements, liturgical practices, governance, social engagement, Church-state relations. There will be things on their long, long lists that they know they have in common: these perhaps can be banked at the outset, clung to as signs of hope. There will be things about them they know are different, but might be negotiable, things that are held lightly and contingently, more lightly and more contingently than they hold to that mandate to unite. There will be things about them they know are different, and there is no obvious way to unite them, and no obvious way to circumvent them, for they are nothing less than the reasons they have been separate all along. There will be things about them on which they cannot even agree whether to differ: sacramental issues on which one participant can easily recognise the other, but not *vice versa*.

Where to begin? Do the representatives immediately grip the issues likely to keep their denominations apart, because if those cannot be overcome the rest of the exercise will be a waste of time? While they have the energy of initial hope and the excitement of appointment to a major task, do they try to knock over those biggest obstacles of all, knowing that the smaller others will be skittled over in the momentum of such a great breakthrough?

Or do they start at the bottom, using their common life as a reassuring foundation, beginning with those bankable common practices, and working upward through the levels of difficulty and improbability, building capacity for the task in each other's company and progressing by slow attrition through the issues? Can either of these possibly succeed?

A hundred years ago the denominations that eventually joined to form the modern Church of Scotland, the Church of Scotland and the United Free Church of Scotland, found a different way to overcome their differences. Their sticking-point was the nature of the relationship of the Church as a spiritual body and the State as a secular power, a relationship on which they had fundamentally different views, in an area of ecclesiology that in a previous generation had produced their original division. Before the stage of detailed union negotiations, the Established Church took several steps to change its own constitutional law and practice. Assembly decisions reflected in Acts of Parliament, the far-reaching re-arrangement of the Church's property, and the translation of the Church's self-understanding into completely different terminology, all these steps were taken first within the Church of Scotland. These actions were taken in consultation with UF partners, but as legal actions they were unilateral, and they would have remained in place if the union had eventually failed in its last stages. Here was a denomination willing to change itself quite apart from the moment of uniting with another, to align itself in advance to another Church's needs in an act of staggering trust and optimism. Perhaps there is no other way to have any prospect of success, when conversations about union too often begin with a depressing list of issues that are not all fixable.

The only other way to achieve union is to settle for the things that are already in common, a 'lowest common denominator' approach that overcomes points of difference by sacrificing them, creating a Church that incorporates some parts of existing Church life and not others. That would be to abandon completely the issues that divide because they cannot be reconciled, and cannot often produce a new Church that is a serious successor to any of its constituent denominations. That would be a thin Church, a shell Church. It could be a destination for the radical souls who have never much adhered to those matters of principle and disagreement in their own Church, and who prefer unity ahead of the traditions that are important to other people; but it would not be a destination for the mainstream of those Churches.

SCIFU illustrated a very human process flaw in these kinds of union negotiations. Over many years a small group of representatives met from the participating Churches, reporting back from time to time to their assemblies and synods and being given just enough encouragement to continue their task (or rope with which to hang themselves, depending on your level of cynicism). These were people long immersed in the ecumenical endeavour, and thoroughly at home with each other, having often worked with each other in that field. In other words they were friends, and consolidated that friendship further during the process; and the SCIFU negotiators as a team became almost like another ecclesiastical entity, another interest group, apart from the various Church bodies that appointed them. Their individual trust was deep, and they had time to understand what each other meant, to hear re-assurances about suggestions in contentious areas, to immerse themselves in each other's thinking. The problem was that these individuals could not take with them into the meeting room the whole membership of those assemblies and synods that would have to approve their plans; so the final say was in the hands of people who had made no part of their journey to trust and familiarity and understanding. On the most difficult issue separating the Churches, patterns of leadership, the team dragged the existing models as close together as their imaginations would permit, and produced a suggestion that still asked a big conceptual step of each participating body. Most of the negotiators were themselves committed to it – certainly all those who had been there since the beginning of the process – because they could see all the steps and turns along the way, and were sure they could come up with nothing better. The predictable veto could have come from any denomination, and it happened to be the Church of Scotland whose Assembly expressed it first. In the aftermath, one school of thought argued that the negotiations should have been stopped much earlier and the time of the ecumenical experts not wasted; that the General Assembly should not have made encouraging noises in the earlier years if its member knew they would reject the final Report. Another school of thought argued that it would have shown a lack of faith to declare at the outset that such a negotiation was impossible, and not to make a reasonable attempt.

If SCIFU, a national effort, failed before any union could take place, the Livingston Ecumenical Parish is a local experiment that sounds a warning even where the united body has come into being, indeed has existed for as long as anyone can remember. Somehow this parish, fully belonging to several Protestant Churches, has a constitution in which each denomination can recognise the necessary elements of its own polity, and a supervisory structure to which each denomination is willing to cede enough authority to keep it alive. Even when things are working tolerably well and running routinely, it takes up enough energy of ecumenical officers and area authorities that it could not be replicated very often elsewhere without the ecclesiastical structures grinding to a halt. Sometimes situations emerge that press on the neuralgic points of difference the constitution cannot resolve – to do so it would have to be as big as the whole Church law manual of each denomination. Then the negotiation of the whole project (it has been variously called an experiment, a project and a parish in its time) has be opened up to some extent, and the texts re-worked by lawyers. No-one has audited the number of hours spent on issues arising from the parish's ecumenical nature, the marginal time-cost over and above the effort needed to sustain and supervise a normal Church of Scotland parish. No-one has devised a calibration of ecumenical benefit, to measure the gains of the current arrangement; and some would struggle even to name them before they are weighed. No-one therefore has been able to judge whether there has been a net benefit, compared with no project at all, or compared with another way of working together.

The Lund Principle

The union model aims high, impossibly high. It is the right ambition only if it is what the Churches believe is meant by the divine mandate for unity. If another model of unity is worth pursuing and is more likely to succeed, how much further would the same amount of energy take the Churches, if re-applied?

The third world conference on Faith and Order at Lund, Sweden, in 1952 issued this challenge:

Should not our churches ask themselves whether they are showing sufficient eagerness to enter into conversation with other churches, and whether they should not act together in all matters except those in which deep differences of conviction compel them to act separately?

This 'Lund Principle' recognises that there are differences of conviction so deep in each Church that to some extent they are compelled to act separately; union, presumably, would be ultimately impossible, however many areas of agreement might be found and celebrated. The Lund Principle requires just as much effort, just as much friendship and trust, as any negotiation for union. The Lund Principle by implication profoundly criticises any two churches offering the same practical service to the same community, radically questions any two congregations separately celebrating the same occasion, challenges the clergy in any community to remove the needless duplication of their work and become effective by pooling their efforts.

In the spirit of the Lund Principle, the Church of Scotland and the Roman Catholic Church in Scotland sustain the little theological gem that is their Joint Commission on Doctrine. Exploring together the doctrinal truths that transcend denominational difference, the Commission has found itself realising unexpected areas of agreement, for example in elements of the doctrine of justification. Pressing the discussions to the point of action, the Commission has produced materials – most notably a new service for the re-affirming together of baptismal vows – that can bring people of such different traditions together comfortably, to take each other by surprise in single acts of worship and encouragement. The JCD is a tortoise in the ecumenical race, moving at what feels sometimes like an excruciatingly slow pace, and taking years on each agenda item. Yet over a few years unexpected results emerge, and perhaps those measurable achievements are greater and more miraculous than the small steps that are taken more quickly, more riskily, around the country.

In the spirit of the Lund Principle, the Churches in Scotland sustain a national body that provides national support and advice for local ecumenical projects and partnerships involving any combination of the participating Churches. In its meetings, united congregations are rarely mentioned; but many other patterns of unity are explained, modelled, urged, supervised and supported. There are parishes in which more than one congregation share a church building; areas of development were several Churches organise joint mission; congregations all over the country where newcomers and visitors are offered an explicit sacramental welcome regardless of their own tradition. The national body saves each of them from having to reinvent their processes, offering sample legal documents, regional support groups, contacts with similar projects elsewhere, and central points of reference and advice.

Who would dare to predict what the effect would be if the Lund Principle were observed by all the leaders and clergy of all the major Churches in Scotland? Its direct benefits would be transforming of church life and clergy stress. In the large town where the Church of Scotland minister is close to breaking point, conducting 75 funerals and 20 weddings a year and providing school chaplaincy in both primary and secondary schools, and the Episcopal and Methodist clergy currently have ten funerals and six weddings each, one can imagine the effect; and in some places it is already done.

The indirect effects in ecumenical relations are more difficult to guess. Perhaps such unity of effort and purpose will persuade the Churches that the differences of governance and sacrament that divide them do not need to be overcome; for the world sees the work they do together first and foremost, and perhaps the world does not mind – or perhaps it even understands – the wealth of their variety, the harmlessness of their distinctiveness. By what right anyway should anyone discriminate against someone who wishes to receive only a Catholic communion, or be baptised only in a Baptist tradition? Or is that attitude a wicked quietism, a failure to be scandalised enough by disunity? So instead would the Lund Principle, fully implemented, help the scales to fall from the eyes of those who maintain the terrible differences among us; and so at last the insurmountable obstacles will look foolish and unnecessary, and be swept away in the tide flowing through all the Churches together?

Ecumenical Instruments

Though the answer to that question is known only to God, and may not be known to the Church in our generation, there can be no avoiding the obligation to know each other, to know and constantly to explore what are the common features that can be shared and exploited, and what are the hopeless differences that have to be circumnavigated. Churches cannot pretend to be doing their best if they are not constantly curious to know what breakthroughs are taking place in other places, that might be adapted, adopted, made to work here where there had seemed no hope of progress. There is, therefore, no avoiding the cost of those expensive networks that bring the churches within each other's earshot for exactly these purposes. Churches gather that have Scotland in common, Britain in common, Europe in common, being Reformed in common, occupying the world in common, and for other traditions there are other bodies.

Anti-ecumenical rhetoric complains about these. Mrs McGlumpher in the back pew has never heard of ACTS, CTBI, CEC, WCRC (actually her minister probably hasn't yet heard of WCRC, so who can blame Mrs McG?) or WCC; so why on earth should her offering help to fund them? Mrs McGlumpher, on the other hand, has never done anything so wicked that she needs to worry herself about any of these. Out there far beyond her back pew, knowledgeable and experienced ecumenical operators will be representing her and half a million others in those listening places, in those places of coming together and discovering things in common and of mourning things that keep traditions apart. They carry the burden of constantly, constantly straining to find the moments in which change can come, change that will not deprive Mrs McGlumpher of all that is dear to her, but change that may make her Church stronger and the whole Church stronger.

Crossing Threshholds

Even without all those special ecumenical efforts, simple practices of friendly curiosity carry great weight. Every Church is enriched by those of its people – leaders and laity – who are willing to visit other traditions. Looking at the other person's scenery, scenting the air, feeling the emotions of their liturgies, tracing the patterns of their devotions: these are the things that create fondness and respect. The Reformed congregation who visit their Catholic neighbours to observe the Stations of the Cross in Holy Week, and the Protestant congregation who receive communion in the Episcopal Church on Christmas morning, they take a tiny step closer, a step that like all steps cannot be untaken. No-one has negotiated anything away, but something human and divine has taken place, and someone is richer. The thresholds of neighbours can become more welcoming than forbidding, as people walk back and forth through them without anxiety or threat. No practices will be transferred – everyone may be thoroughly confirmed in their different habits – but one group can learn to give thanks for what enriches the other, and may be secretly enlarged by the experience for all they know. And that is easiest between congregations in separate denominations, where the differences are clear and no-one needs to be confused about their own Christian identity. Visiting someone else is not frightening when home is secure and familiar and accessible.

Ecumenism inside the Church of Scotland

The most difficult challenge in Church unity must be the divisions that exist within traditions. Debates as difficult as the one about human sexuality expose some of the cracks, dig deep into them and create wide fractures. How much easier it is where those fractures split the body completely, and each part can move forward in its own unity. Easier, and yet it is the outcome so much institutional energy strives to prevent, the outcome that is assumed to break God's heart. Does it really? That rather depends on the answer to that question that lies behind all the other ones; whether God minds the Church having many and more denominations. Would two Churches, each free from a suffocating enveloping by this issue, really do less good in our country than the one Church that is dominated by an unseemly, distracting argument?

The cultural and theological differences in the Church of Scotland are wider than the differences between some of its parts and other Churches. The aeon of difference between a liberal, high Cathedral-tradition congregation and a conservative, evangelical parish church will be far wider than the differences between the first of those and its Episcopal neighbour, and between the second and its local Free Church.

There was once a Presbytery faced with neighbouring congregations ripe for union, each with a building large enough to hold a united congregation, located two minutes' walk apart. The theological instincts of the two could scarcely have been more contrasting – the man on the Clapham omnibus might have been surprised to discover that they belonged to the same denomination – and the wise Presbytery had the courage to decline to unite them, finding other ways to manage its local resources. There was once, though, another Presbytery faced with neighbouring congregations located so remotely that neither could ever be united with any third congregation; and it had to be union with each other or none at all. The theological instincts of the two were again profoundly different, and the helpless Presbytery felt bound to unite them even in the teeth of bitter opposition. Time will tell whether it was worth it.

The Church of Scotland has not split – or only has not yet split, for all we know – because the protagonists cannot decide what should split it. There are too many issues on which we disagree with the each other, and too many combinations of opinions on different sides of different arguments. If those issues are all of roughly equal importance, the lack of a dominant fault-line about one disagreement will keep the national Church together as a single entity, to the extent that it is a single entity. When one issue dominates all the other arguments, like-minded people will group round that point of principle, so committed to it that they will be able to live with the other differences that distinguish them from each other. Then a piece of the Church will be able to break off, itself containing disagreements on many things but with a headline issue on which all agree together. That will be painful, unattractive, expensive, scandalous. It will also be liberating, relieving, permission-giving, reviving – for both sides. We do not know who would be in such a fragment, for it could come about in several ways including ones that no fool would claim to predict. Whoever each may be, gone will be the need for either side to keep making room for the other across impossible differences.

The church union model that demands so much energy in the inter-church movement has the same exhausting effect inside a Church that is dangerously broad and diverse. If parts of a Church cannot quite be themselves, be true to their convictions and pure in their beliefs, because they are bound with others they cannot endure, that Church may one day realise its width was unsustainable. Fragmentation and the re-union of fragments from different old fractures to form new alliances and bodies may be the natural and traditional Scottish way of being the Church, creating new possibilities by losing old tensions, freeing souls who could not live together any longer, bringing together souls whose previous ecclesial organisations had been needlessly keeping them apart.

What are the things that must never happen? Secession? Disruption? Division? Mustn't they, ever?

Winchester Cathedral has a massive West window that looks as if it belongs to the heyday of twentieth century visual art. It is a mass of shattered stain glass, a beautiful blur of colour that illuminates the stone-work inside the building without constituting any picture. In fact it dates from the seventeenth century, when the old stain glass was smashed in the religious wars of the era, but its tiny shattered pieces built again into something new, something that waited 300 years before it looked as if it might have been designed to be that way.

Pen portrait

There was a nasty little niggle spoiling their joy when the baby arrived. Everything was fine, really, and both sets of parents were so enjoying being grandparents for the first time. The wee one seemed to have decided on a pretty tolerable routine, and really they were all getting the hang of it surprisingly well.

They'd really enjoyed the conversations they had about the future. It was part of what made them such a strong couple that they held just the very same views about what they wanted in life; so sharing their dreams about the things they wanted to teach the wee lass, the opportunities they wanted to give her, the kind of thoughtful person they wanted her to become, that was *so* important.

The problem was the baptism. They had talked about religion very seriously when they first got together, and found they had the same attitude. Each had come from a church-going family, and both had great respect for their local parishes. They could see what a comfort religion was for many people, and they agreed it was an important part of community life. They were happy to go along from time to time, especially on big occasions like Christmas and Easter and especially Remembrance; and they were pretty generous with their offering on those occasions. In all honesty, though, neither of them was ever going to sign up to the whole package and become a member, or have communion, or anything like that.

So his mum's very pointed questions about baptism dates were really becoming an issue. Mum wasn't meaning to be difficult, because it was all very important to her and – sure – she wanted to give thanks in her own way for such a big gift in her life. It was just that she seemed to have less respect for the meaning of baptism than they did themselves; while she thought they should just get on with it whatever they might happen to believe themselves, they would never take vows they knew they wouldn't mean. It had all the makings of the kind of disagreement that would last for ever.

So thank goodness they'd had the courage to speak to the minister of the church up at the traffic lights, where they'd been to the Watchnight Service last winter. Steven had come along for coffee and he'd been wonderfully understanding. He seemed to agree more with their way of thinking than with Mum's – or at least he seemed to respect it more than she did. And in the middle of their apologies and explanations he came up with this thing they'd never heard of before, a service of thanksgiving for the baby. It wouldn't be a baptism, and it wouldn't prevent her being baptised later on. It wouldn't involve any vows that would make them uncomfortable. It would be a great celebration, a chance for the more religious members of the family to thank God and promise their love and ask for blessings on the new life.

What they liked most about Steven, after they had pounced on his suggestion and accepted it with huge relief, were the two questions he asked before he left. First, would there be a party afterwards and could he come? And second, would they like to invite him back for coffee next time Mum's visiting?

The First-Time Commissioner

(WHAT THEY CAN'T TELL YOU AT THE TRAINING EVENING)

For every minister and deacon, and for many elders, there will one day come a first commission to serve in the Church's General Assembly. Your experience on the Kirk Session (and, usually, on Presbytery too) prepares you only a little for the size, purpose, colour and solemnity of the Church's biggest court; and it is easy to feel rather daunted and overwhelmed.

Make sure that your Presbytery Clerk arranges for you to be invited to the social and information evening for first-time commissioners, normally held the night before the opening session. Guided by Assembly officials, you will work out where to find everything, discover how the technology works, hear something of how the debates are run and – more important than any of those – meet about 150 other first-timers in exactly the same position as you. Your feelings of confidence will rocket, and you will have all the help you need. You may also receive a DVD that reinforces that guidance, and describes some of the procedural information you will need to understand. What follows tries not to duplicate those two sources of help; but perhaps it may assist you further, filling in some truths the official versions could not possibly include.

What you're there to do

In a week so intense that you will return to your normal busy life for a rest afterwards, you will find yourself in four kinds of activity.

Governance is the purpose of the Assembly, its legal function. This is the body that makes the Church's national decisions; so it is the business of the Assembly that produces its measurable outcomes. It is your highest priority in the week, and you should never be asked to do anything else during the business sessions, however worthwhile or attractive.

Worship and ceremonial give the Assembly its unique character, rooting all its work in its Christian confession and re-affirming its relations to the culture and community of Scotland. Your programme will not suffer any clashes at the key moments of opening and closing ceremonies, communion, and Sunday worship.

Education and information are increasingly offered to commissioners through the ever-expanding Assembly 'Fringe', events provided by the Church's agencies and outside bodies and held in the spaces between other kinds of business, especially at lunch-time or at the end of the working day. This festival of the Church's life is a bonus in your week, but attendance at its events should never take priority over your diligence in the formal business sessions.

Social contact is a vital strand of your Assembly experience. You may find yourself invited to official events hosted by the Moderator or the Queen's representative (the Lord High Commissioner), and these will be carefully fitted within the official timetable to enable you to do everything. On these occasions you will be able to get to know the delegates and visitors from other Churches, who make up about 10% of the Assembly's membership, bringing the friendly perspective of other traditions to the work of the week. But as elders make new friends and meet old ones, and as ministers and deacons catch up with university contemporaries and old colleagues, the week becomes a time for strengthening ties across Church and country. Conscience must guide you when the competing demands of duty and opportunity collide and there are too few hours in the day.

Of the four elements, the business of governance absorbs your preparation time and poses the many challenges of understanding what you are there to do and how you go about doing it.

The Church of Scotland, for fascinating historical reasons, has its own legal system so that it can regulate the spiritual aspects of its life without any interference from the civil law. The only way to continue to merit that independence is to have all the elements of a complete system; and those must include a legislature (to make the rules), an executive (to implement the rules) and a judiciary (to enforce the rules where necessary, and to resolve problems and disagreements). In the United Kingdom, you will find these elements respectively in the Westminster Parliament, the departments of government and civil service, and the courts of the land. In the Church of Scotland you will find the equivalent elements in the General Assembly in its legislative mode, in the agencies working out of 121 George Street and elsewhere (which account to the Assembly for their work), and in the standing Commissions of the Church (which exercise the Assembly's powers of judgement). Even more than in Parliament, then, the General Assembly is the point of authority for each part of its own legal system. As a commissioner, you will have to exercise authority in each area, and each of them requires you to make decisions of policy. No wonder you have such a lot to learn.

One comfort is that the Assembly in recent years has devolved almost all of its judicial functions to smaller, more effective, more specialist bodies. The most technical cases, therefore, are unlikely to come your way. The very few cases that still come to the Assembly involve the most controversial issues of principle; and if you find an Appeal on the Order of Business, prepare to see the public queuing down the Lawnmarket in anticipation.

Whatever the business at hand, you have been commissioned as a member of the General Assembly for the same reasons you were ordained to the ministry, diaconate or eldership in the first place; that a spiritual quality was recognised in you that qualified you to make decisions and determine the Church's policy. You have been sent because the Church believes you can think and decide and choose. So you should be firm about two things, and resist many people who will try to persuade you otherwise. First, never ever carry a mandate on any issue from your congregation, Kirk Session or Presbytery. Second, do not finally decide your own mind on any issue until it is debated. If your Presbytery or Kirk Session attempts to direct you how to vote, have them stopped. And what is the point of the written reports, the passionate speeches, the daily worship asking for the inspiration of the Holy Spirit; what is the point of the process if your mind was made up a month ago, if the minds of others who do not have the information you have are controlling your actions? Our Assembly teeters on the brink of having theological 'parties' campaigning one way or the other. With one or two sad exceptions, our Church resists that temptation most of the time. May we retain enough open minds that those debates, those prayers, those pivotal moments of persuasion in each Assembly will always matter.

Your commission to the Assembly disqualifies you from complaining about any decision it has made unless you went to the trouble of speaking and voting against it. Gone is your right to complain about things done 'by 121'; for 121 is simply there to implement your decisions as an Assembly. Abstaining will not help you, because in our tradition abstentions are not counted (the leaders of a Christian Church – and that's you whether you think so or not –are expected to come prayerfully and diligently to a mind on each issue), and your failure to vote is nothing more than a failure to try to prevent the policy from being adopted. The burning issues of the Church's life are being put before you, and you have to decide what to do.

How it's done

Most of the information you will need to have to allow you to make informed and intelligent decisions is contained in the Blue Book, which arrives at your home about four weeks before the Assembly begins. Set aside about two days, around three weeks before the Assembly, to read the whole thing, and you will still have enough time to explore with experienced local ministers and elders the material you have found more difficult to understand, or discover the background that will make sense of it.

Be prepared to play to your strengths, and enjoy the Reports that resonate with your experience. If you have lived in the Middle East, you will probably find something in the Report of the World Mission Council that intrigues you or makes you want to make a contribution to their debate. If you have strong feelings about the professional development of our ministry, the Ministries Council Report will seize your interest. If you are passionate about the Church's built heritage, a more technical Report like that of the General Trustees will fascinate you. Remember, though, that you will have the responsibility of making decisions on all the subjects of the week, and read through everything, even if you feel you are not expert in all of it.

At the beginning of each Report, find a shaded box containing its Proposed Deliverance. It is a Deliverance, because it is a set of decisions the Assembly can deliver to the Church (and especially to that Council or Committee which will then have to implement them). Crucially for your reading, it is only 'proposed' at this stage, because the Council or Committee has suggested here what it would like the Assembly to decide about its work. But the Assembly are the bosses, and will decide what the Deliverance will finally contain. Some people will be naturally distrustful of a Proposed Deliverance, though that depends perhaps on the source of the Report, and they will assume it is the Assembly's task to reach a final Deliverance very different from the original proposal, much more demanding or critical of that committee. Most people, though, trust their agencies, the decision-makers who serve on them and the professional staff who service the work, and largely agree with the proposals given. The debate in the Assembly does not start from a blank sheet of paper; but as in the well-run Presbytery you may already serve, it starts with the Proposed Deliverance and the Court decides whether and how to change it, a lot, a little, or often not at all. What, then, do you feel is not right about it? What, most interestingly of all, is missing from its terms but vital for the Church to grasp?

That just leaves the week itself, and the business on each day.

In many places (e.g. see the introductory Church law materials on the Church's web-site, or the DVD mentioned earlier) there are descriptions of the order of debate: how to tell apart different kinds of motion, in what order things happen, what is out of order completely, how the reporting conveners are able to reply to the discussion, and so on. You will find that the Moderator keeps order very clearly, and a good Moderator will enable newer commissioners to make their points even if it is obvious that they are not yet experts in the process. And if you are planning to make a contribution and have questions about the method, speak before the session begins to someone at the Clerks' table in the middle of the Hall. These men and women are to Assembly procedure what the guy in the small business locally is to your home computer: the questions you are facing for the first time, and the processes you have never tried before, are the bread and butter of the Clerks, Business Conveners and lawyers, and they will untangle you in an instant. Because they serve a court, they dress ceremonially and try to look serious; but really they are expert pussy-cats, and delighted to be given a problem to play with.

If you are going to be a useful servant of the Assembly, taking a lead in its work and changing other people's opinions, there is nothing for it but to speak. Your second contribution is much easier than your first, whether the two are separated by a few hours or a few years; but there is no way to reach the second one whilst avoiding the first. The General Assembly contains only two sorts of people: the ones who once upon a time made their first contribution and know how you are feeling; and the ones who have yet to summon up the courage and are in awe of you. You will be well received if you pick a subject on which you know something and speak briefly, seriously and politely. So do it, and get it over with. Then your duck will be broken, and you will have found your place in the heart of the Church's governance.

If you are unsure about any of this, find a Youth Representative. You can normally identify them by their age... These creatures are frighteningly well prepared, the more experienced training the newer, and all of them studying the Reports together each evening and helping each other to contribute. Beyond the Assembly's staff, this group is more likely than any other to know exactly what is happening, and how to make something new happen too. They know how to do it.

How not to do it

You will be tempted to learn at the feet of the masters, those commissioners who are clearly old hands at the Assembly and seem to have figured out how to make it work for them. Some individuals just seem to main-line the whole event and it brings them to life. These frequent flyers make dangerous models, some of them, and there are habits you would do well not to learn.

Half a dozen commissioners in each General Assembly have never learned the Law of Diminishing Returns. Do you remember, at school, when you were swotting for an exam and working out how much work you had to do to get the result you wanted? 20 hours of study would probably get you a bare 50% pass-mark, but it would take 30 hours to get 60%, and it might take 50 hours' work to get 70%. As the grade increased, each mark took more additional effort: the return diminished as the effort increased.

In the Assembly that law works like this. The Commissioner who in the course of the week makes just one carefully-judged contribution on a topic that interests them will be heard with great interest and respect, and will quite possibly help to determine the decision that is made. The Commissioner who makes two contributions per day will arouse slight suspicion, and it will be assumed he or she is trying to be noticed. The Commissioner who makes half a dozen contributions each day makes everyone else's heart sink, wastes everybody's time and irritates the reporting Conveners. This Commissioner, poor chap, probably thinks he (I can't think of a recent female culprit) does have particular wisdom to offer to his 800 colleagues on each particular topic, every single time. He also thinks he is a much-loved character, even poorer chap.

There is a cure. The Moderator has on the screen in front of him a list of those wishing to speak, and is under no obligation to select speakers in the order in which they have asked to contribute. If you, the first-time commissioner, realise that in fact you do have something fresh and helpful to say, and your name is on the Moderator's list, he will be delighted to call you, rather than 'no-show-without-Punch' who is itching to speak... again.

An associated addiction is that of attending the Assembly, quite unnecessarily, every year. There are Presbyteries to be easily found where it is difficult to fill the complement of commissions, sometimes because the Presbytery does not exercise strict enough discipline over working ministers who do not realise that attendance every four years or so is part of their job and not a matter of choice and taste. And there are members of Presbytery who are quick to fill those places, because they enjoy the Assembly so much, or perhaps fear it cannot quite manage to make the right decisions without them.

There are also Presbyteries labouring under the carefully-maintained impression that it is necessary to send the Presbytery Clerk every year to the Assembly, so that he (again I can't think of any female culprit) can better perform his job. They are too polite at the introductory evening to say it, so let it be said here: there is absolutely no need for any office-bearer of any lower court to come to the Assembly every year. The Assembly is web-cast, and all the paperwork the Presbytery needs is sent to everyone afterwards; so Clerks and others are more than adequately resourced for their own work. If a Presbytery is able to fill all its commissions, then the perennial attender will block a place that might allow a younger minister or newer elder to attend for the first time.

If a commission were built on a mandate from Presbytery, so that you were told how to vote on the important issues, it would matter less if the same people went each year. But since commissioners cannot be mandated, and must make up their own minds, our polity is designed with the expectation that all our leaders will take their part in due turn in the work of our supreme Court.

Those are issues about quantity of contributions, but problems arise too about the quality and style of debate, especially when the speaker is opposing the position of the reporting committee, represented in the Assembly by its Convener. The underlying error is to forget that everyone present is on the same side in the mission of the Church; and some commissioners debate as if the Convener is there to be bested, overcome, defeated. A conversation in advance, a suggestion talked through with the committee's officials to find out what is practically possible, a motion crafted in terms the Convener can happily accept, a gracious speech commending the area of work and persuading the Assembly of this excellent further development, a friendly reply by the Convener, and approval by acclaim by the Court; these present an elegant and constructive way to advance the Church's labours.

Two sorts of tactic present the opposite impression. The first, which one might call 'ambush', involves the commissioner keeping her powder dry and saying nothing in advance about the motion she wishes to bring. Nothing appears in the printed list of Notices of Motion, and the Convener and committee staff have heard nothing of it. Suddenly, at the appropriate point in the debate on the Proposed Deliverance, the commissioner springs up and brings the motion as a hostile act. The Assembly officials are put in a flurry as they try to enter it into the minutes (because part of the commissioner's tactic has been to fail to give notice to the Clerks, knowing they will do the Convener the courtesy of passing it to him). The committee's officials are wrong-footed, because they are not armed with the information they need to explain why the proposal is not achievable, or affordable, or high enough among their existing priorities. The Convener is simply infuriated, and being human too is likely to suffer a visceral reaction against the proposal, however attractive it might otherwise be.

The tactic often fails. The inability of the staff to find justification to resist the proposal means, obviously, that they also do not have the evidence to allow them to support it. The Convener knows more about the general policy direction than the wee nyaff making the proposal, and can usually respond with enough lofty oratory to squish her. The Assembly, above all, has a strong corporate sense of decency and courtesy, and enough imagination to feel what the Convener is feeling. The Convener normally wins, when there was no need for the idea to fail.

There is one scenario in which the ambush tactic can succeed. Very, very occasionally, a Convener somehow manages to annoy the Assembly, evading reasonable questions or being ill-prepared or making a poor attempt to distract the Court from something his committee has done without Assembly approval. The Convener has a weakness, and jolly well deserves for it to be exposed. Then the killer contribution, made without warning to trap the Convener, would indeed be fatal, probably fatal to more than just one debate.

It nearly happened some years ago, when the Convener of a large Council was asked a question relating to a trust fund closely related to his area of work. The question was a pointed one, in a controversial area. The Convener's reply was that he and his Council members could not possibly speak for the trustees of the other fund, and a very proper and legally correct answer that sounded too. By a common failure of nerve, or a reluctance to destroy the Convener's credibility there and then, none of the few people present who knew the truth pointed out that the Convener and his senior Council members were themselves the trustees of the fund *ex officio*, and could perfectly well have answered the question. But that is, at most, a once-a-decade event; and normally ambushes deserve to fail.

The second tactic, almost the converse of the first, might be called 'attrition'. Here the commissioner uses two sorties to achieve victory where one should do. Questions are always in order throughout the debate, and the commissioner asks a question clearly designed to open up the topic of her choice, draw the Convener into revealing his response to her argument, and begin to build up sympathy amongst fellow-commissioners. When the correct point in the debate arrives for the motion, the commissioner moves her amendment or counter-motion, and makes what is effectively the second half of her set of arguments, attempting to demolish the Convener's answer to her earlier question (when I say 'earlier', it may at worst have been only a few seconds ago, where the commissioner is not remotely adept at this).

The Assembly's collective and unspoken irritation this time relates to the wasting of its time. Were all commissioners to speak in the course of the week, just once each, there would not quite be enough time in the Assembly time-table for all the contributions. Bad enough the commissioner described earlier with no instinct for the law of diminishing returns; but worse by far when a member of the Assembly makes the same argument twice in quick succession, abusing the facility for questions to be asked for clarification. Here the brave Moderator, once he has grasped the authority he ought to be wielding, should do whatever it takes to remove such duplication, and rule out of order any question that is clearly part of this tactic. Such authority applied unapologetically a few times would have a transforming effect on some people's behaviour.

Follow your own instincts of courtesy, and the Golden Rule, and you will soon accord with the mind of the whole Assembly and understand its responses.

How it's all reported

The Assembly Press Office is a major operation in its own right, and wearies of the unvarying complaint 'there's less media coverage than there used to be'. That means: day-time TV did not exist 25 years ago, and the test-card space was replaced with dreary live coverage of Assembly debates, which addicts could watch for hours. It means: the national papers are more secular and less sympathetic to the Church, and feel less of a duty to report the annual showcase of an organisation with less than 10% of the population in its membership these days. It fails to notice, on the other hand, that modern instant communications have enabled regional papers to carry much better daily coverage of issues relevant to their area. It fails to notice the web-streaming of the whole event (of far more than even day-time TV of old could cover).

Perhaps, as a first-time commissioner yet to make your mark, you could do or say something in an Assembly debate that was worthy of media attention? Perhaps it is the commissioners' responsibility to be noteworthy and interesting.

No-one who writes about the Assembly or tries to introduce you to its ways can predict whether it will inspire you or leave you cold. There are indeed ministers who do everything to avoid attending it, and some members who leave it none the wiser than when they came. There are certainly young leaders in the Church, including some ministers, who were immersed in the Assembly as Youth Representatives and were fired up in their Christian journeys by the experience. There are certainly elders who love to return, knowing they will learn more about the national Church in this one week than in a lifetime of local service. There are certainly ministers and deacons who feel lifted out of the routine of their work and reminded of challenges and causes beyond their usual duties.

If you are asked to go, take the chance.

Pen portrait

The Convener is sitting so far back in the East gallery that she is almost invisible. Since she is not a Commissioner this year, this is the first day she has attended this Assembly, and it is a little hard to tell whether watching the other debates in today's order of business has helped to attune her head to the mood and pace, or just made her nerves worse.

There is a certain amount of comfort in the preparation she has been able to make. The Committee secretary has been through the speech with great care, and obviously has confidence in its style and tone. It won't take up the whole twenty minutes allocated, and since the committee is such a small one that will go down well. The clothes are right, and they will make her feel she's coping and make the Assembly sense she's in control. Most of all, her head is full of last Friday's session with the staff: every possible question, surely, has been thought of, and crisp, credible, honest answers have been worked out.

In the bowl of seats below her is a strange mixture of Church people. Some she knows personally; faces she sees in her own Presbytery, and even – right at the back in the long row under the clock – her own minister thoughtfully positioned in line of sight from the Convener's lectern. Some she knows by reputation; figures who recycle from place to place and committee to committee all over the Church. Some make her heart sink a little, like the minister who gave her predecessor such a hard time last year and who somehow is here again with ominous scribbles all over today's blue Assembly papers. And there is the elder who sent the three letters full of irritating, stubborn questions to the Secretary earlier in the year; and he's kneeling beside the chair of the Vice-Convener of the Business Committee, earnestly discussing a text being typed onto the computer screen down there. Well, if it's the same old gripe, the same old failure to grasp the point, at least there's the chance to make the explanation once and for all to the whole Church, nail it down finally and be done with it...

And then, suddenly somehow, the Convener is sitting in the chair beside the Moderator. A glass of water is beside her left foot, and her folder of answers is beside her right foot. In her hand is a sheet of A4 paper just handed to her by the Depute Clerk, and sure enough the counter-motion to section three of the committee's

Proposed Deliverance, from the predicted source, is precisely what they all anticipated at the very start of last Friday's conversation, practically word for word. Above and behind her she knows her husband sits with the Moderator's husband, and if this morning was anything to go by he will be more nervous than she is. To her right, in the front row of seats, the members of her committee give her encouraging little nods and smiles. The first excursion to this lectern may after all be rather good fun.

The Left-Handed Minister

I have set the Lord always before me. Because he is at my right hand, I will not be shaken.
    Psalm 16:8

I wonder how many lists would be produced if everyone in a congregation was asked to write down the things they do not have in common with the person in the next pew. There would be lists of physical features and lists of mental abilities. There would be lists of domestic circumstances and lists of professional achievements. There would be lists of relationships, lists of likes and dislikes, lists of faults and failings and lists of qualities. I wonder what sort of list would be produced if everyone in a congregation was asked to write down the things they know about each other that should disqualify the other one from ever being ordained as a minister. The outcome would depend, of course, when you were asking. In a certain country in a certain age the list would include black people. In a certain country in a certain age the list would include women. In a certain country in a bygone age the list might include left-handed people.

It is startling to check the number of occurrences of the phrase 'right hand' in the Bible, and find they are ten times more than the appearance of 'left hand'. Discount the instances where the left and right hand are treated simply as a pair without distinction, and the difference is twenty-fold. When the Psalmist sings of the mighty achievements of God, they are achievements of the divine right hand, which is responsible for all that is powerful, triumphant, holy and righteous. The left hand of God is never credited with any of that. Honour is awarded by the gift of sitting on the right hand of a throne. Just as Solomon honoured Bathsheba by installing her at his right hand in the Old Testament, so in the New Testament Jesus' final place of triumph is at the right hand of God. In the same way the righteous and blessed sheep in Matthew 25 – those who fed the hungry and visited the prisoners and tended the sick – were placed at Christ's right side, while the wicked and cursed who failed to do these works of kindness were consigned to his left. Matthew's story had no need to specify those placements: the separation into two groups would have made the point without rubbing it in.

And for much of Christian history in Western culture the obvious inference has been drawn, in the language of what is 'right' and what is 'sinister', of 'rectitude' and of 'gaucheness'. In a more enlightened modern age we no longer mean to make a moral comment by that vocabulary; but it is common enough still to meet men and women who remember being taught to write with their right hands against their instincts. I can think of an intelligent woman now in her 40s who was denied the chance of violin lessons at school because she would have been the only left-handed child in the tuition group (a fact that would have been to her advantage in learning fingering).

Is it not therefore a colossal stroke of luck for ten percent of the population that the Church has never found itself inferring that left-handed people are not suitable to be ordained as clergy? Women, black people, albinos and Jews have all been painted as inferior human beings at some time; so why on earth have lefties got off with such a distinctive characteristic? These are men and women who we now know usually have their brain hemispheres reversed. They are, surely, slightly different creatures from us normal people, and it is very easy to imagine the kind of line that might be drawn, a line that would keep them on the outside. And yet, by an accident of history and despite some dicing with popular culture and the education system of a not-very-bygone age, they have managed to keep status as normal men and women.

By doing so they deprive the rest of us of a most convenient social tool to celebrate and affirm our own normality. René Girard's philosophical anthropology insists that we recognise the liking of our societies for a scapegoat. Girard's provocative theory of the Gospel - Jesus the victim of the mimetic desire that produces scape-goating violence, but exposing and so overcoming it - goes much further than the point I want to make. We can see easy scapegoats in families, workplaces and, yes, churches. We see them wherever there is unease and discomfort and a need to be rid of its cause. The family pulls together wonderfully as the harmless son-in-law is divorced, demonised and denied access to the grandchildren. The firm senses a new lease of commercial life when the manager is sacked as if last year's results were his fault. The congregation relishes its greater purity when the elder who asked all the awkward questions finally resigns in protest.

Those doing the persecuting have something new in common, something easy to agree on and easy to measure. They scarcely need to find anything positive to talk about, because they have a common horror over which they can shudder together, a common enemy they can plan together to defeat. For the length of time it takes to expel the impurity from their midst, that group has a bond that matters more than all the things that separate them from each other. If they are fortunate, it might take years and years to get rid of the unwanted presence, years and years when they can define themselves in terms of that battle and cluck together over the terrible danger in their midst. In their efforts organisation will emerge, strategies and structures to support their cause. Leaders will arise whose oratorical skills will ginger up the faithful and remind them of their duty; perhaps even increase the overall fervour and take just a little further the lengths to which everyone else will be willing to go. And since the cause is so fervently espoused in one community it will doubtless exist in another, wherever the same kind of misfit needs to be removed from fitting in at all. Networks will develop so that communities can encourage each other, commend each other, compare purity and strategy and leadership. The leaders will interact with each other and the leaders of leaders will be identified, anointed, appointed. And in all these communities of people engaging with each other in such complicated tasks, power and influence will begin to become a feature of the common effort. With its internal structures of authority growing as the movement gathers momentum, terrible power of destruction will be wielded on the victims of the process, who may have done nothing more than want to sit on any seat in the bus in 1960s America, or quite literally go about their business in 1930s Germany.

> *If I forget you, O Jerusalem, may my right hand forget its skill.*
> Psalm 137:5

How does it feel when we claim the Christian life but acknowledge that we have belonged to such a group, or know that because we are fallen humans we so easily could? By the failure of moral courage that is at the root of so much sin, we long to belong to the main crowd and never to look or sound different. We adopt our opinions on goodness and badness, rightness and wrongness, as a herd. We are convinced by whatever is the standard attitude now, this year, among these people. We are like teenagers who follow fashion and deeply scorn the fashions of the previous decade, while their parents know perfectly well that but for the accident of their date of birth the kids would have happily worn the platform shoes and the mullets. In our moral immaturity we gain confidence from sharing in the hostility of the majority towards the outcast. We take pleasure when someone no-one likes fails or falls. We triumph in the decisions our organisations make that affirm us in our majority view, as of course they would.

After the Lord Jesus had spoken to them, he was taken up into heaven and he sat at the right hand of God.
Mark 16:19

All of this works only if the scapegoat is weak enough for the scapegoating to work. Two obstacles can get in the way of a really good persecution. The first is the failure of the community to pick on a minority small enough to bully. You could have predicted, as soon as emancipation came to America's slaves, that it would be only a single lifetime until there were too many free black men and women to put up with legally-enshrined white supremacy. While it is common enough for discrimination to be practised against enormous social categories by hard-core bigots, it is difficult to sustain that behaviour by a whole society and authorise it in law. The minority has to be small enough.

The second threat to this sinful social process is the moral courage of a few heroes amongst the majority. They refuse to join in with the hostility, put themselves among the persecuted group, break the unwritten social code of society and offer themselves as alternative scapegoats. They mess with the heads of the immoral majority, daring them to turn their fury on them though they do not fit the bill, do not present the abnormality, do not manifest any human inferiority. It may come in heart-warmingly simple terms, as it did when a class of primary children took to spending each interval break chasing one girl round the school building, calling her names and making wild and improbable threats. (She came from a home where personal cleanness was obviously not a priority, and she was taller than the others and awkward. You might almost, in the spirit of this piece, say she was gauche. She was certainly sinister, in the minds of her classmates.) About two-thirds of the way through the year one other girl in the class became fed up of feeling uncomfortable and guilty about the daily routine, and suddenly befriended the victim, who had the grace and forgiveness to let her. Within a day or two the pursuit had stopped, since after all there was no fun in it any more and no reason to chase them both. On a scale too huge and distracting to fit into a short essay, every programme of accompaniment by brave individuals in places of persecution and injustice has this same aim, beginning with Christ's friendship with lepers, prostitutes and tax-gatherers and continuing today in places that still include Palestine.

When the terror stops, because the victims stand for it no longer or there is just too much moral courage in the air, the community is healed of its tear and has to return to a far more difficult pattern of life, picking up all the tricky little issues that make routine existence so complicated, issues it was so good not to have time to be irritated by when there was an important cause to distract and unite everyone.

That is what the Church of Scotland must have experienced in the late 1960s when women fought their way into the eldership and ministry, leaving those who had said 'over my dead body' puzzled to find they were still alive, and still facing all the other, more important challenges to modern Christian witness.

Women were more deeply problematic than left-handers would have been to keep out of Church leadership. A left-handed person could have been promised that he would be ordained just as long as he started writing with his right-hand. A woman finds herself in an incurable condition that cannot be resolved by counter-intuitive behaviour and by pretending to be something she is not. A left-handed person would have been able to resist the use of Scripture by inference to demonise him, pointing out that there is no direct condemnation in any particular verse. Women were faced by St Paul's direct proscriptions, and had to make sophisticated arguments from hermeneutics to make the case for a different rule in an utterly different society. A left-handed person belongs to a minority of about ten percent of the adult population, just few enough that the Church knows it could carry on with that number excised from its ministry. Women constitute at least half of the membership of the Church and would always remain visibly present to ask the embarrassing question.

Not that discrimination against women is unjustified in all circumstances. Even today women do not serve in front-line infantry roles, or in Royal Navy submarines; and whether those policies are right, or whether the state has just not got round to enhancing resources and altering conditions to allow those distinctions finally to disappear, the differences remain. What had to be overcome in the Church of the 1960s was instead the use of illegitimate arguments to sustain what was familiar against what was right. The 'ugh factor' argument could not be named in intelligent debate, but often lay (and still in communities unfamiliar with the effects of the 1968 Act still lies) beneath the visceral resistance to a ministry that is too far from people's normal expectation.

> But Israel reached out his right hand and put it on Ephraim's head, though he was the younger, and crossing his arms, he put his left hand on Manasseh's head, even though Manasseh was the firstborn.
> Genesis 48:13-15

I have toyed, perhaps just a little sarcastically, with how the Bible might have been interpreted if conditions and temptations had been just a little different in the course of Christian history. I refuse to descend into the debate about how the Bible ought to be interpreted on any particular issue; for that is a hopeless task amongst people starting with such different interpretative principles that they might as well be talking different languages. It seems to me, though, that our Church opened an important door 40 years ago. It chose, as an institution, to do something a significant minority believed was contrary to an explicit instruction in the New Testament, because it resolved that the argument had many other elements and should not be closed by just that one. It engaged with questions of women's ordination on the basis of asking *why* something was written, and not merely accepting *that* it was written. A precedent has been set; and if the Church were, say, to consider outlawing left-handed ministers, it would be deeply inconsistent not to ask the same contextual questions and acknowledge similar underlying principles of fairness and equality.

And so where are the Church's left-handed or female or black or disabled ministers left by all this? What is their duty? It is, I am sure, the universal Christian duty of humility and purity. In humility each created child of God can scarcely presume they could have anything about them that would authorise them to speak about or for God. If there is a line to be drawn and below it are those not qualified to speak of grace and divinity, then do not we all acknowledge in the fearful middle of ourselves that we lie below that line? Do we dare to invite inferences about ourselves when we disparage any other?

And what is our purity for? What does it serve? What is its measure? One person, comfortable with sexual abstinence, is squeamish even at the thought of the most faithful, noble married love. Another, wracked by multiple sclerosis, does not feel pure in his mind unless he has cannabis in his system. Another, in all conscience, cannot eat meat. Is any harm done by the most rigorous self-discipline, self-denial? No, and respect will be given by those who admire the consistency of principle from a position of personal freedom to come to their own conclusions about their own lives. The woman who declines to be ordained for reasons of theological conviction, and whose decision was personal, informed and unbullied, can only be held in high regard; and all that should be asked of her is that she holds in equal regard those who have come to a different conclusion and followed a different path. Is harm done when one person's idea of purity is imposed on another's living or believing? Yes, and terrible sadness when a life with all its talents and skills, experience and wisdom, relationships and emotions, is counted as nothing because of something that has never stopped the flourishing of all these qualities.

It takes courage, does such self-knowledge; and time and space we rarely apply to the exercise. It takes wisdom, does such discernment of the goodness God would have us pursue for the world's sake. It takes humility, does such confessing of what makes each different from her neighbour; stronger in one way and weaker in another. It takes dignity, does such unapologetic insistence on following the calling of God no matter what someone else thinks of your purity, your suitability, your eligibility to answer the calling you are sure you hear.

> When I saw him, I fell at his feet as though dead. Then he placed his right hand on me and said: "Do not be afraid. I am the First and the Last."
> Revelation 1:17

Pen portrait

How fast will it fade? When I come back here in a year's time, in five years' time, will I feel what I feel now as I drive along this road? Will my hands twitch on the wheel because I'll feel as if I ought to stop at that cottage there, where the wee lad came as such a surprise to his mum who didn't realise she was expecting for the first five months? Will my stomach do a little jump when I drive past that farm, and think of the terrible accident that took away such a fine elder? Will I slow down on the corner there to see if I'll get a glimpse of that first bairn I ever baptised, growing up so fast she makes me feel old?

Or will it be just a relief, to take that invisible back-pack off, that responsibility to care about these people without stopping, without knowing when the next phone call can't be ignored, when the schedule is broken up by someone else's tragedy? But I'll pick up a new load, when the induction to the new place happens next week; and the only difference is I don't know where the needs are up there. That mental map of people's stories and connections, the births and relationships and enmities and deaths and histories, it will have to be built all over again in a new place.

And what about this place? What will they say when Sunday is over with all its goodbyes, and we are finally gone? Will they all be heaving a sigh of relief, and resolving to make sure the next minister is completely different? Will they remember the funerals? The weddings? Anything I said? Anything I taught? Will I meet the children in future years and be remembered by them?

And how will they do?   Will the Presbytery allow them to call another minister straight away? Will they get on with building that new centre on the car park, or was that only me shoving them from behind? Will they manage to do the fund-raising for that? Will Jessie throw her usual spanner in the works in the Board meeting, and persuade them all it's a hopeless ask and a waste of their time and a silly imposition on folks' good-will? Or will Paul manage to fire them up even though he's so young, and make them feel ambitious, and tell that story again of his dream for the new building and the good that can be done there?

What will it look like, then, when candidates come for interview? A creative building-site with a buzz of ideas to be sorted out and grasped? Or exactly as it is now, neat and quiet and perhaps just a little dull?

And who will do Jim's funeral, which can't be far away now? I hope Tom will be able to take it when the time comes, because he'll know what to say about Jim's church work, and his adoration of his wee grand-daughter, and the pride he took in his herd. Ach now, don't be thinking of that; soon it will be none of your business.

Lightning Source UK Ltd.
Milton Keynes UK
15 May 2010

154183UK00002B/7/P